Michael Grow is an associate professorial lecturer in history at George Washington University. He is also affiliated with the Woodrow Wilson International Center for Scholars, under whose auspices he has written a *Scholars' Guide to Washington, D.C. for Latin American and Caribbean Studies*. He received his B.S. (1966) and M.A. (1968) from the University of Wisconsin, Madison, and his Ph.D. in history (1977) from George Washington University.

The Good Neighbor Policy
and
Authoritarianism in Paraguay

United States Economic Expansion
and Great-Power Rivalry in Latin America
during World War II

Michael Grow

THE REGENTS PRESS OF KANSAS
Lawrence

Library of Congress Cataloging in Publication Data
Grow, Michael.
The good neighbor policy and authoritarianism in Paraguay.
Bibliography: p.
Includes index.
1. Paraguay—Foreign economic relations—United States.
2. United States—Foreign economic relations—Paraguay.
3. Latin America—Foreign economic relations—United States.
4. United States—Foreign economic relations—Latin America.
5. World War, 1939–1945—Economic aspects—Latin America.
I. Title.
HF1524.5.U6G76   337.730892   81-11
ISBN 0-7006-0213-5

To Linda

Contents

List of Illustrations

List of Tables and Graph

xi

Introduction

Although the final days of World War II found the nations of the Western Hemisphere united in opposition to the "Axis powers," wartime relations between the United States and Latin America were complex and—more frequently than has generally been recognized—discordant. Complicating the equation of inter-American relations during the war was a diverse mix of ideological, political, economic, and security-related factors—factors which produced radically differing, and at times conflicting, perceptions of "national interest" among United States and Latin American policy-makers.

Ideological factors. The Latin American policy of the United States during the late 1930s and early 1940s was formulated and implemented against the backdrop of a global struggle between two rival ideological systems—the democratic/capitalist institutional models of Anglo-American liberalism and the totalitarian/statist models of European fascism—as the proponents of each system proselytized and propagandized in an effort to attract adherents to their respective models elsewhere in the world. In Latin America, this external ideological competition between liberalism and fascism was superimposed upon an internal Latin American environment itself characterized by conflict between several distinct ideological variants, including: (1) a "liberal" variant, whose adherents traditionally identified with democratic and capitalistic institutional structures; and (2) a "radical right" variant, whose adherents included (a) indigenous fascists openly espousing radical totalitarian experiments in their respective nations and (b) "authoritarian nationalists" bitterly antagonistic to liberal structures and advocating dictatorial and statist solutions to domestic socioeconomic and political problems. Latin America's ideological pluralism assured that, in an international military confrontation between the Anglo-American "democracies" and the Axis

1

nations, each side would receive support and sympathy for the morality of its cause from a substantial sector of Latin American public opinion. Inextricably tied to ideological considerations were political factors.

Political factors. Latin America's internal ideological conflicts took place primarily in the arena of national politics, in the form of domestic power struggles between rival liberal and rightist "power contenders." Pitting liberal elements, who were closely identified historically with British and United States interests in international affairs, against rightist elements, who were deeply impressed by German and Italian experiments in national development and who in many cases had close personal links with German Nazis and Italian Fascists—these power struggles had significant implications for the formulation and implementation of foreign policy in each Latin American nation, as well as for United States policy toward each of those nations. Indeed, the shifting configurations of political power within the internal political systems of Latin America —as liberal factions and rightist factions competed to control their national governments—produced an ever-changing spectrum of obstacles and opportunities for United States policy-makers in their efforts to forge a unified U.S.-led, pro-Allied coalition of hemispheric allies during the war. Conversely, domestic politics in the United States exerted, at most, a secondary influence on the course of inter-American relations, owing probably to the strongly bipartisan stance of the Republican and Democratic political parties on foreign-policy issues throughout the war.

Economic factors. Central to the perceptions of United States policy-makers was a Depression-induced need to restore employment, production, and prosperity in a domestic U.S. economy crippled by the events of 1929 and after. In the context of hemispheric foreign policy, this goal translated into a concerted U.S. effort, undertaken in the face of direct German economic competition, (1) to expand export markets in Latin America for United States industrial products, (2) to defend and enhance the position of private United States investment capital in Latin America, and (3) to maintain secure access to Latin American natural resources and raw materials. Latin American policy-makers, for their part, sought with equal determination (1) to protect and expand all of the existing commercial markets—in Europe and Asia, as well as North America—available to their fragile export-dependent, raw-materials-producing economies; and (2) to stimulate—if possible, by means of economic assistance from the leading industrial nations of the Northern Hemisphere—the process of economic diversification and domestic industrialization which they believed could eventually free their domestic economies from monocultural export-dependence and vulnerability to unpredictable, devastating fluctuations in international trade, such as those of 1929/30. Harmony in inter-American relations during World War II required a reconciliation of these frequently contradictory goals of national economic self-interest.

Security factors. United States officials perceived of several potential hemispheric threats to U.S. national security, among them: (1) that one or more of the Axis nations was planning a military invasion of the Western Hemisphere, and thus constituted a direct menace to the territory and population of the United States; (2) that Germany would conquer Britain, France, and the Netherlands, and transform the Caribbean possessions of those European nations into a new German colonial empire on the vulnerable U.S. southern flank; or (3) that Germany, by means of fifth-column tactics (utilizing German immigrant communities in Latin America) and/or manipulation of local Latin American rightist elements, would create a dependent bloc of Latin American client states, governed by pro-German puppets, as an enclave for further German expansionism in the hemisphere. Latin American officials, by contrast, tended to define their national-security concerns during the war less in terms of defense against potential Axis aggression and more in terms of a calculated geopolitical expediency. Functioning in a highly competitive international environment which had always been dominated militarily and economically by stronger "great powers" from the Northern Hemisphere, and confronted now with a cataclysmic global power struggle between rival coalitions of the leading great powers, Latin American policy-makers deemed it essential, for reasons of national security, that they secure an advantageous and comfortable position for their respective nations in international affairs by remaining on good terms with *whichever* great power or group of powers seemed most likely to achieve a dominant position in world affairs during and after the war. United States and Latin American leaders thus tended to approach the issue of an "Axis threat" from distinctly different perspectives.

───────

The following case study evaluates the relative influence of these various factors in shaping United States wartime relations with Paraguay and the neighboring republics of southeastern South America, a region which contributed most significantly to the tensions in inter-American relations during World War II. It should be stated at the outset that, although four categories of variables in the inter-American equation (ideology, politics, economics, and security) have been isolated herein for expository purposes, the boundaries which separate these categories are by no means distinct or well mapped by contemporary scholarship.

Indeed, such concepts as the interrelationships linking politics and economics, the relative degrees of significance attached to political values and economic principles within ideological systems, and the importance of economic factors in perceptions of national security remain vaguely defined among students of inter-American relations. Nor should the emphasis placed upon ideology, politics, economics, and security be taken to imply that these were the only causal factors in the equation of inter-American wartime relations. Although relegated herein to a secondary position of explanatory significance, such factors as "bureaucratic politics"—that is, competition and conflict among the various administrative agencies within each national government for power and influence over governmental policy—and the idiosyncrasies of individual human nature—for example, a United States diplomat's outrageous personal behavior overseas, a Latin American diplomat's personal ambition to gain his nation's presidency, a Latin American president's emotional attachment to his handicapped son—cannot be ignored as significant elements in the process of foreign-policy decision-making among the nations involved.

Finally, it was considered insufficient to focus solely on questions of *causation*, without a concomitant examination of *consequences*. It became apparent during the course of research that the policy actions of some of the nations studied had a profound impact on the subsequent course of events in others of those nations, and that in several respects the patterns of tactical interaction which the United States and the republics of southeastern South America developed in dealing with one another during World War II had a major influence on the nature and style of subsequent interactions between them after the war. Accordingly, the concluding chapters of this case study focus on the impact and legacy of wartime relations in terms of the nature of the inter-American relationship during the postwar era.

1

Domestic Responses
to the Great Depression:
The United States and Germany

As the United States and Germany struggled to overcome the crippling economic stagnation of a massive world depression during the 1930s, each nation sought to revitalize its dormant domestic industrial production by acquiring new foreign markets for its manufactured exports. By the middle years of the depression decade, this search for new markets had led the two industrial powers into an intensely competitive trade rivalry in southeastern South America.

A populous, underdeveloped, agricultural region with few native industries, southeastern South America constituted an attractive potential market for United States and German industrial exports. For more than a century, the nations of the region—Argentina, Brazil, Paraguay, and Uruguay—had been closely tied economically to an older industrial power—Great Britain—exporting their raw materials and agricultural products in exchange for British manufactured imports and relying in large part on British investment capital to develop their public utilities, their transportation and communication networks, and their banking structures. To supplant Great Britain as the leading industrial trading partner of southeastern South America became a component part of the economic-recovery programs of both the United States and Germany, and by the mid 1930s, the two nations were actively competing with one another in a drive to lure the region away from the British economic orbit.

In the United States, the presidential administration of Franklin D. Roosevelt inherited a national crisis of unprecedented proportions as it took office in March 1933. So severely had the U.S. standard of living

5

been eroded during the three and one-half years since the financial collapse of October 1929 that the very survival of the nation's political and economic structures seemed in jeopardy. The great U.S. experiment in national development through liberal institutions—the framework of pluralistic political democracy and free-enterprise capitalism that had produced a stable political system and a prosperous, expanding, industrialized economy in the decades since the American Civil War—appeared close to failure in 1933. Between 1929 and 1933, the nation's gross national product had fallen by 29 percent, industrial production had declined by 54 percent, and the vitally important steel industry had been reduced to operating at a mere 12 percent of its capacity. Falling production figures led to rising unemployment levels, and the 3 percent of the U.S. labor force without jobs in 1929 had swelled to over 25 percent by 1933. The resultant human suffering in turn had given rise to violent protest marches and food riots that seemed to call into question the ability of the elected national government to meet the essential needs of United States citizens. The crisis continued to worsen until, on the eve of the presidential inauguration of 1933, the nation's banking system virtually collapsed, and the very heart of United States capitalism —the New York Stock Exchange—suspended operations.[1]

Roosevelt immediately sought to restore public confidence in the nation's political and economic institutions. In his inaugural address he proclaimed his faith in "the future of essential democracy" and his confidence in the ability of the "stricken Nation" to endure, revive, and prosper.[2] In office, he quickly launched his early New Deal recovery program, a series of temporary emergency measures designed to arrest the economic decline and reinvigorate the free-market economy—"to energize private enterprise," as Roosevelt phrased it.[3] To combat the Depression, the new administration expanded the role of the national government in the domestic economy. First, the activities of the nation's financial community—the "unscrupulous money-changers" of the banks and stock exchanges—were brought under strict governmental regulation. Then, to coordinate production and raise profit levels, Roosevelt persuaded business and labor to accept greater centralized governmental direction under a system of licenses and codes, offering business a suspension of antitrust laws and freedom to engage in price-fixing, and guaranteeing organized labor improved bargaining rights and work benefits. At the same time, he launched a program of massive federal spending to stimulate the productive base and the consumer market. In a deliberate pump-priming effort, the administration injected several billion dollars of governmental funds into the economy through credits and subsidies to banks, farms, and commercial establishments, loans and mortgages to private individuals, and welfare relief and public-works job programs for the unemployed. Such measures marked a significant increase in the powers and responsibilities of the national government in United States economic life—in essence, a major step away from laissez-faire capitalism and toward state capitalism. Nevertheless, Roosevelt had not lost faith in traditional free-market capitalism. He had not, for example, resorted to the nationalization of banks and industries as did the leaders of several other capitalist nations during the Depression. Instead, he sought to rehabilitate U.S. capitalism through governmental stimulation and regulation, temporarily assisting and, where necessary, disciplining the private sector, restoring consumer demand and business confidence in order to revive and preserve the basic fabric of the nation's free-enterprise economy.[4] "It was this administration," he later boasted, "which saved the system of private profit and free enterprise after it had been dragged to the brink of ruin."[5]

In its immediate impact, however, Roosevelt's early New Deal succeeded only in stemming the tide of further economic decline. It proved ineffective in turning the economy around or in bringing about a return to pre-Depression levels of prosperity. Industrial stagnation and mass unemployment persisted obstinately, despite the administration's recovery efforts. And as a consequence, Roosevelt turned increasingly to the realm of foreign policy in seeking remedies for the nation's continuing economic malaise. During 1934, he formulated an international economic policy designed to stimulate domestic production by opening new overseas markets for the nation's foreign trade, which had plunged from $10 billion in 1929 to $3 billion in 1932.[6] The new international economic policy was initiated in February 1934, with the creation of the Export-Import Bank, a government lending agency empowered to grant low-interest credits to foreign governments for the purchase of United States exports. The heart of the administration's new policy, however, was the reciprocal trade agreements program, launched in June 1934. Designed to expand foreign markets for United States products by reducing tariff barriers in international commerce, the reciprocal trade agreements program permitted Roosevelt to negotiate bilateral international trade agreements which offered reductions in United States tariff rates on foreign imports in return for a reciprocal lowering of a foreign nation's customs duties on United States goods. To multiply, or multilateralize, the anticipated increase in international commerce that was expected to follow, each reciprocal trade agreement was to include an "unconditional most-favored-nation" clause automatically extending the specified bilateral tariff reductions to any other nation that similarly agreed not to discriminate against United States products.[7]

As a vehicle for reviving the U.S. economy, the administration's new foreign economic policy was a consistent and complementary counterpart to its domestic recovery program. Just as Roosevelt, in his domestic policies, had mobilized the national government to channel extensive federal assistance to the private sector of the economy in an effort to revive the free-market system, so he now proposed to mobilize the government's resources in foreign affairs for the same purpose. Government funds in the form of Export-Import Bank loans would prime the pump of the international economy, subsidizing increased foreign spending in the United States to the direct benefit of United States manufacturers, traders, and shippers. At the same time, the administration would attempt, through its reciprocal trade agreements program, to forge a liberalized system of world trade, in which barriers to free commercial intercourse between nations would be eliminated in favor of an international free market with multilateral "open doors" for unencumbered trade relations. In its immediate impact, such a program would increase world trade, creating more markets for United States manufactured exports, in turn stimulating United States industries to reopen their idle factories and expand their dormant production, thereby reducing unemployment. In the longer-range future, Roosevelt's program would create a liberalized international economic environment of unrestricted free competition, in which United States private enterprise and private capital, once rehabilitated to their former prosperity and dynamic assertiveness, could be expected to gain a position of preeminence and thereby assure the continuing economic growth that would safeguard the United States from any future depression. By the end of 1934, equipped with its new tactical international economic plan for domestic recovery, the Roosevelt administration thus turned its attention outward in a search for new trading partners and expanded foreign markets, a search that would lead to a growing United States interest in the nations of southeastern South America during the second half of the decade.

Along with the United States, Germany was the other industrial nation most severely crippled by the world depression.[8] Already reduced in status from a major world power to a second-rank nation by its military defeat in World War I and the $33 billion in war reparations punitively imposed upon it by the victors, Germany had already endured a difficult period of acute postwar depression and inflation lasting into the early 1920s when the international financial dislocations of 1929 struck its economy. Then, between 1929 and 1933, German national income declined by a precipitous 34 percent, while industrial production fell by

42 percent, and unemployment rose from an already alarming 10 percent of the labor force to 37 percent.[9] By 1932, one out of every three German citizens was living entirely or in part on charity or relief.[10] The democratic parliaments of the Weimar Republic proved to be utterly ineffective in ameliorating the crisis, and as living conditions deteriorated, the German people turned for salvation, not to a rehabilitation of Weimar liberalism, but to the ideological prescriptions of fascism, elevating Adolf Hitler and his National Socialist movement to power in January 1933. In doing so, Germany committed itself to a radical new experiment in national development, one that was openly hostile to liberal institutions and antithetical to the liberalized international economic system that the United States had determined to promote.

Fascism attracted great interest throughout Europe in the two decades following World War I. Europe had emerged from the war in a devastated condition, only to be buffeted by severe postwar inflation and then, after 1929, by a massive depression. As the capital savings of the middle classes were destroyed and urban workers and rural peasants descended lower into the depths of propertyless poverty, the parliamentary democracy and industrial capitalism of European liberalism became steadily more susceptible to attack, particularly from an increasingly radicalized labor movement that engaged in violent strikes and called for the overthrow of the prevailing liberal order in favor of a new international workers' society. This threat of proletarian class revolution had taken on an imminent reality with the Russian revolution of 1917 and the subsequent efforts of the Soviet government to mold the trade-union movements of the world into a revolutionary Communist International. In this tense atmosphere of economic distress and political unrest, fascism appeared, offering an ideological panacea, a new system of national development, to rescue Europe's nations from liberalism and protect them from communist revolution.[11]

Fascists blamed liberalism for Europe's postwar maladies, charging that its excessive emphasis on freedom of action in both the political and economic spheres had brought the European nations to the brink of uncontrolled anarchy by permitting narrow group interests to assert themselves at the expense of national well-being. The results of capitalism seemed, to the fascist, everywhere apparent: an industrial revolution under arrogant capitalists who ruthlessly exploited burgeoning masses of destitute factory workers; giant industrial monopolies and business trusts that crushed small middle-class entrepreneurs and gouged consumers; unregulated financial speculation that led to periodic stock-market crashes and ruinous depressions. The results of democracy seemed equally apparent: ineffectual parliamentary systems of corrupt

9

politicians, squabbling political parties, and selfish private-interest groups that had factionalized the political process to the point of chaos at the very time when each nation desperately needed strong, unified leadership to overcome economic catastrophe. But liberalism's ultimate sin, from the fascist perspective of the turbulent postwar years, was that it had intensified the very conditions of political divisiveness, economic inequality, and class hostility that facilitated the spread of revolutionary international communism, a movement which—with its cross-national call for class warfare by the workers against their oppressors, its stress on international working-class solidarity, and its foreign organizational direction—threatened not only to violently overturn established social structures but to imperil the very existence of the nation-state as the traditional, historic organizational base of Europe's cultural communities in favor of an internationalized world proletariat headquartered in Russia.[12]

As an ideological alternative to liberalism and communism, fascism propounded a revolutionary totalitarian nationalism. "Nationalist revolutions" led by patriotic national elites would overthrow discredited liberal regimes and establish totalitarian dictatorships, restoring political and social order and launching coercive state-directed programs of national economic recovery and social reform that would thwart the appeal of communism. Identifying with, and appealing to, idealized national traditions of fatherland and historic cultural uniqueness, each fascist dictatorship would instill in its fragmented society a unifying spirit of patriotism and selfless dedication to national progress. Once unified through nationalism, the nation would be collectively mobilized and regimented for an intensive campaign of economic development under the technical coordination and discipline of the directing fascist elite.[13]

As an administrative apparatus appropriate to a non-Marxist totalitarian dictatorship, fascists seized upon the device of the corporate state. The concept of corporatism, as handed down from medieval European philosophers by way of nineteenth-century Catholic social theorists, perceived of human society as a living organism composed of functionally interdependent "corporate" organs—variously described as estates, social classes, or interest groups—each of which performed an essential function or role in the social "body." According to corporatist theory, when these corporate units functioned together in interdependent harmony, the result was a healthy society enjoying organic solidarity and internal stability. When they did not, the resulting internal disruptions and inner conflicts could have fatal consequences for the social order. The industrial revolution of the eighteenth and nineteenth centuries

10

produced just such inner conflicts in European society, in the form of increasingly complex and fragmented social structures, class antagonisms, and violent industrial strife. In response, various nineteenth-century European political philosophers resurrected corporatist concepts in a search for measures to restore class harmony and stability in their discordant societies. By the early twentieth century, intellectual movements in several European nations[14] were calling for the creation of new "corporate states," in which society would be integrated together in a stable, harmonious, functionally interdependent framework. Specifically, the corporate-state concept proposed to group all economically active individuals in society into broad occupational categories—labor, business and industry, the professions, and so forth—and establish for each category a guild-like trade association, or "corporation," possessing autonomous jurisdiction over its own internal affairs and primary responsibility for unity and discipline among its members. Each corporation, as a major economic interest group, was to be represented in a national corporative council or chamber—an economic parliament that would replace the geographically represented parliament as the main legislative and consultative branch of national government. Impartial state arbitration would resolve all disputes between corporations on the basis of equal justice and the national interest.

To fascist theoreticians of the post–World War I period, the corporate state was an ideal administrative mechanism for achieving class reconciliation and social harmony in socially fragmented nations without disrupting the existing social structures. By giving antagonistic elements in society, including the alienated workers, equal functional representation in governmental structures through corporate interest groups in which they could articulate and defend their specific interests, the corporate state would reintegrate a class-torn society and negate the appeal of communist class revolution. More collectivist than individualistic liberalism and yet more integrative than class-divisive communism, the corporate state would reorder society into disciplined, collective, functional sectors which, under the totalitarian control of a fascist dictatorship, could be efficiently subordinated to the national interest for a regimented campaign of state-directed economic recovery and growth.[15]

Fascism was a supremely developmentalist ideology, as befitted a movement born in a period of catastrophic world economic crises. From the fascist perspective, the international economic system was a ruthless and dangerously unstable arena, crowded with nations competing for wealth and status. In such a world, fascists believed, only those nations that efficiently mobilized their resources and energies for the maximum development of national economic strength were assured of survival and a position of invulnerability and prestige in international affairs. To this end, fascism's approach to economic recovery and development was shaped by a profound economic nationalism, which took as its goal maximum feasible national autarky—a closed, self-contained industrialized economy self-sufficient in manufactured goods and raw materials, separated and insulated from the unpredictable international economy and thus invulnerable to its violent fluctuations and cyclical depressions. To achieve autarky, fascist dictatorships would dramatically expand the state's regulatory power over the private economy, replacing the free-enterprise capitalism of the prevailing liberal state with a new totalitarian state capitalism, in which private enterprise would continue to exist, but under a pervasive state control designed to purge it of its exploitative "profiteers" and "parasites," its "rapacious capitalists" and "financial gangsters," and harness it to serve the state's development program.[16] Totalitarian state control would extend over every aspect of the nation's economic life, including wages and prices, production and distribution, credit and investment. Foreign trade, in particular, would be brought under strict state management, and nationalistic trade mechanisms would exploit the international economy for the purpose of achieving national autarky. High tariff barriers and foreign-exchange controls, for example, would protect the nation's developing industrial and financial interests from foreign competition. A state trading agency would monopolize the nation's exports and imports, manipulating their flow to the benefit of domestic industrial expansion and self-containment. Bilateral barter agreements would secure raw materials unavailable domestically but necessary for industrial diversification and self-sufficiency.[17] As a formula for economic development, the fascist program of totalitarian economic nationalism—stressing autarky, a closed, self-contained economy, pervasive state controls, and discriminatory trade restrictions—constituted a serious challenge and obstacle to United States plans for an open, liberalized international economic system of unencumbered multilateral free trade between nations.

Fascism's promise of political order, social harmony, and economic progress, couched in a patriotic appeal to nationalism, found responsive audiences throughout Europe in the unsettled aftermath of World War I. Various elements among the upper classes saw in a stabilizing fascist dictatorship a device which, subverted to their own control, could be used to suppress popular unrest and protect vested property interests from the growing threat of communism. To many workers whose nationalist sentiments had been strongly reinforced by national military service during the war, the fascist call for economic progress and corporative functional representation was, with its uplifting appeal to patriotic nationalism, more persuasive than international communism. But fascism attracted the majority of its adherents from among the middle classes— the desperate consumers, small shopowners, and independent farmers who saw in its promise of state regulation and economic recovery a salvation from the ruinous depressions and exploitative, monopolistic workings of industrial capitalism that were rapidly undermining the middle classes' hard-earned economic independence and threatening to force them back into the propertyless lower classes from which they had arisen. By the onset of the world depression, no European nation was without its vocal fascist movement lauding totalitarian nationalism and fascist dictatorship as the panacea for national recovery and regeneration.[18]

Fascism achieved its first major success in Italy in 1922, when Benito Mussolini rose to power on a program calling for an Italian "nationalist revolution" to restore order, discipline the vested interests, provide social reforms for the lower classes, and rebuild Italy into a power of significance in world affairs. By the 1930s, Mussolini had consolidated his dictatorial powers and had begun to extend a web of totalitarian state regimentation over every sector of Italian society—controlling the press, the courts, the police, the schools and youth groups, forcefully welding the once-autonomous labor unions into a single docile, Fascist-controlled corporate federation, cautiously eroding the economic independence of the powerful aristocrats and industrialists, and eventually replacing Italy's parliament with a corporative chamber under a new corporatist constitution.[19]

Fascism was to have its most dramatic impact, however, in Germany. There, beginning in 1933, Adolf Hitler's National Socialist government aggressively aggrandized dictatorial powers in order to overcome the Depression and free the nation from "the chains of Versailles" by building an indomitable and economically invulnerable new Teutonic Reich. Under Hitler's demagogic leadership, the German state assumed unlimited powers of control and regulation in economic affairs through arbitrary decrees such as the one which declared that "any German resident who, consciously or unconsciously, moved by base selfishness or by whatever vile sentiment, contravenes legal rules and causes grave prejudice to the German economy, may be condemned to death and his fortune confiscated."[20] The productive sectors of German society were quickly divided into corporate "estates." Private capital was brought under total state control, with powerful government control-boards regulating the financial community and the industrial sector. A single government-controlled Labor Front replaced the existing trade unions, and its "Strength through Joy" program rewarded cooperative

13

workers with government-subsidized housing and low-cost vacations. Government subsidies aided the recovery of German heavy industry, while massive government-financed public-works programs built new highways and railroads, providing jobs for the unemployed, stimulating industry, and developing the modern transportation network necessary for further internal expansion. Foreign trade came under pervasive state direction, with the government assuming direct responsibility for securing essential raw-material imports and new export markets for German industry, most notably in eastern Europe and southeastern South America.

The initial results of Hitler's totalitarian recovery program were impressive. Within six years, while the United States continued to languish in the grip of industrial stagnation and mass unemployment, Germany had virtually overcome the Depression. Production and consumption were revitalized to self-sustaining levels, industrial output increased by 97 percent, national income by 35 percent, and foreign trade by 25 percent, while unemployment was eradicated so effectively that an acute labor shortage soon developed.[21] To political leaders elsewhere in the world struggling to overcome their own domestic depressions during the 1930s, fascism's impressive initial record of accomplishments in Germany suggested that perhaps nationalist revolutions and corporatist dictatorships were indeed the "wave of the future" in national development.

2

Domestic Responses
to the Great Depression:
Southeastern South America

The Depression opened a deep ideological rift within the ranks of the traditional ruling elite of southeastern South America. Since attaining independence early in the nineteenth century, the nations of the region had been controlled by small upper-class oligarchies of rural landowners, urban commercial interests, military officers, and Catholic Church officials, who together effectively monopolized power, wealth, and property in the region. During the nineteenth century, these oligarchies had conformed to world trends by experimenting with liberal political and economic institutions, hoping to emulate the impressive material progress being achieved in Great Britain and the United States under such institutions. New national constitutions, modeled on that of the United States, established representative democratic governmental structures throughout the region, although the ruling elites carefully safeguarded their dominant position by equipping their chief executives with virtually dictatorial "emergency powers" and imposing restrictive voting qualifications that effectively disenfranchised the lower-class peasant majorities in their societies.[1]

In economic affairs, they turned to the prevailing liberal principles of laissez-faire free-enterprise capitalism and unrestricted international free trade practiced by the more advanced industrial nations of western Europe and North America. In an era when Great Britain, the leading industrial power of the nineteenth century, and the other industrializing nations of the Northern Hemisphere were seeking new sources of raw materials—the minerals and fibers required for their mills and factories, the foodstuffs to feed their rapidly growing industrial working classes—the landed elites of agricultural-exporting southeastern South America saw in unrestricted international free trade an irresistible opportunity to expand their export markets and usher in an era of unlimited prosperity for themselves. Rather than developing domestic industries and diversified national economies, they instead eagerly committed their nations to a subordinate role within the established international division of labor—as suppliers of raw materials for the industrialized world. They deliberately linked their national economies in a free-trade relationship to Great Britain and its industrial competitors, expanding and modernizing their ranches and plantations to produce a growing volume of the beef and mutton, cotton and wool, wheat and sugar and coffee that the industrial markets craved, and trading them for the manufactured commodities—the iron and steel products, chemicals, finished textiles, and luxury goods—which the industrial nations were so eager to sell and which southeastern South America lacked the facilities to produce domestically. At the same time, the industrial world was seeking profitable new investment outlets for its accumulating surpluses of liquid capital, and the elites of southeastern South America, seeing an opportunity to modernize their underdeveloped nations without risking their own financial resources, offered foreign capital an attractive investment climate free from taxation and restrictive governmental controls. The result was a massive influx of British investment capital in the region, totaling some 630 million pounds sterling by World War I. Private British capitalists constructed and operated new banks and import-export houses, public utilities, railroads, telegraph networks, storage warehouses, processing factories, packaging plants, modern port facilities, and trans-Atlantic shipping lines—bringing modern technological efficiency to the outward flow of the region's agricultural exports, opening new markets for British industrial commodities, creating new profits for London stockholders, and in effect transforming the nations of southeastern South America into informal British economic colonies.[2]

Liberal institutional structures served the region's agrarian oligarchies well for several decades. With the responsibilities of their new laissez-faire liberal states limited largely to preserving internal order, protecting private property, servicing the flow of exports and imports, and providing an open door for foreign capital, the expense of maintaining large state administrative apparatuses was avoided. Representative political structures provided a façade of modern, enlightened government, beneath which the established social hierarchies and class inequities were maintained with the traditional repressive force. If governments were frequently corrupt, with rival oligarchical factions vying for the spoils of office through small, fractious political parties, the system occasionally displayed a certain openness and mobility, peacefully assimilating an emergent urban middle class into the prevailing structures by absorbing its nascent political parties into the political process and imbuing its members with elitist social values and aspirations. Free-trade policies opened the way for such a massive increase in the region's foreign commerce during the second half of the nineteenth century that customs duties alone provided sufficient revenues to finance national budgets, making taxation of the landed elites or foreign capital unnecessary, and leaving ample surpluses for political graft as well as a modicum of schools, hospitals, and urban beautification projects for the privileged sectors of society. Meanwhile, high world prices and a steadily growing foreign demand for the region's agricultural commodities brought vast wealth to local landowners, and the commercial operations of the new foreign enterprises opened lucrative new administrative and managerial positions to the elites.[3]

Although key sectors of southeastern South America's economic infrastructure fell under the control of foreign capital, and although the region's growing overdependence on overseas export and import markets dangerously increased its vulnerability to sudden fluctuations in world trade, such conditions found few critics among the prospering oligarchies between the mid nineteenth century and World War I as the international economy experienced an unprecedented era of uninterrupted stability and growth. Beginning in 1914, however, world commerce was to be buffeted by nearly two decades of almost continuous dislocations, with devastating consequences for export-dependent economies. World War I briefly severed southeastern South America's ocean transport links with its European markets, plunging the region into a short but severe recession. The war was immediately followed by rising inflation and a worldwide depression in agricultural commodities that persisted throughout the 1920s. The financial dislocations of 1929 and the ensuing world depression then totally undercut the prevailing international economic order and its free-trade structures. As the economies of the industrial nations contracted, world markets for raw materials dried up, and southeastern South America's export economies virtually collapsed. By 1930, Argentina's foreign trade had shrunk by more than one-half and Brazil's by two-thirds, as Europe curtailed its meat and grain purchases and world coffee prices plummeted from twenty-three cents per pound to eight.[4]

Economic catastrophe produced political unrest, and the post–World War I decades were to be turbulent ones—not only in southeastern South America but throughout the Latin American and Iberian cultural world. Indeed, it was during this period that the Iberic world felt its first revolutionary stirrings of lower-class unrest. Throughout the 1920s and early 1930s, the Spanish and Portuguese parliamentary republics were rocked by Communist-led strikes, peasant land seizures, street riots, church burnings, and assassinations, while in Latin America, local Communist and Socialist parties and militant, anarchist-led trade-union movements made their first significant inroads among the previously unpoliticized lower classes. In traditionalistic, largely preindustrial societies such as those of Iberia and Latin America, however, it was not the lower classes—which were already inured to a subsistence-level existence on the fringes of the market economy—but the propertied upper and middle classes who suffered the sharpest decline in their standards of living during the economic disruptions of the interwar period. Consequently, as incumbent national governments throughout the Iberic world fell into bankruptcy and struggled ineffectually to maintain public order, meet government payrolls, and provide relief aid, they also faced a rising tide of political unrest from among the propertied elements in their societies, as frantic agricultural and commercial interests demanded emergency financial assistance, salaried middle-class employees publicly protested their declining purchasing power, and unpaid military and police forces plotted rebellions.[5]

In response to the crises of the interwar period a number of native Iberic fascist movements appeared, including José Antonio Primo de Rivera's Falange in Spain, Rolao Preto's National Syndicalist movement in Portugal, Plínio Salgado's Integralist party in Brazil, and Juan Bautista Molina's Nationalist Youth Alliance in Argentina. Totalitarian fascism never came to power in the Iberic world, however. Instead, its appeal was co-opted, and its proponents were eventually absorbed, by a dissident "radical authoritarian" faction of the ruling elites—a faction which itself adopted many of fascism's ideological and stylistic trappings, while rejecting its totalitarian regimentation and pervasive state control over all aspects of national life in favor of a more limited, conservative authoritarianism designed to restore national political and economic order while leaving established power hierarchies untouched and intact in the hands of the traditional entrenched elites. "Radicalized" by post–World War I economic breakdowns and social unrest, discontented elitist coalitions of military officers, Catholic Church officials, and conservative intellectuals gradually became convinced that stern and extreme new measures were needed to rescue their nations from economic bankruptcy and impending class violence. Nationalistic army officers, many from the rising middle classes, began to develop a messianic vision of their role in society in the years after World War I, concluding that in such times of national crisis it was the patriotic "mission" of the armed forces to replace ineffectual civilian regimes with efficient military dictatorships that could restore stability and impose the military virtues of discipline, hierarchy, and obedience upon their troubled societies.[6] Sectors of the Catholic Church saw in a paternalistic Catholic corporatist dictatorship a bulwark against the spread of atheistic communism among the lower classes.[7] To traditionalistic elements of the intellectual community seeking an indigenous solution to the growing problems and complexities of the twentieth century, corporative authoritarianism seemed more in harmony with the Iberic cultural heritage than the alien ideological tenets of liberalism or the revolutionary Marxism that loomed as the alternative.[8] Coming together in the 1920s and 1930s, this heterogeneous coalition of alienated conservatives turned enthusiastically to the concept of "nationalist revolution" as an appropriate, and indeed an essential, response to governmental paralysis during national emergencies, while corporatist dictatorships in turn seemed to offer an effective mechanism for correcting the dysfunctions that threatened to destroy their traditional socioeconomic systems. Throughout the interwar period, as a result, these dissident "conservative revolutionaries" of the Iberic world were rising up to overthrow incumbent governments and replacing them with corporatist, authoritarian dictatorships designed to restore order, arrest economic decline, and safeguard their societies from the threat of leveling, Marxist social revolutions: in Spain, under General Miguel Primo de Rivera (1923–30) and again under General Francisco Franco (1936–75); in Portugal, under Antonio de Oliveira Salazar (1926–73); in Argentina, under General José Uriburu (1930–32) and under Colonel Juan Perón (1943–55); in Brazil, under Getúlio Vargas (1930–45); and in Paraguay, under Colonel Rafael Franco (1936–37) and under General Higinio Morínigo (1940–48).

A number of small, vaguely defined authoritarian movements had crystallized in southeastern South America during the 1920s, drawing intellectual inspiration from such earlier antiliberal traditionalist philosophers as the Uruguayan José Enrique Rodó and the Argentines Manuel Gálvez and José Ingenieros. When the devastating impact of the 1929–30 world crisis struck the region, a majority of the directing elites chose to remain loyal to their established liberal institutional structures, hoping to preserve the façade of democratic processes that provided their political parties with patronage and spoils and to restore international free trade and the agricultural export markets on which their wealth and affluence depended. Dissident authoritarian elements, however, now rose up to challenge their liberal brethren for control of national affairs. Disgusted by breakdowns in public order, bitterly resenting economic policies which had left their nations so disastrously at the mercy of international trade disruptions, and fearful that rising currents of lower-class unrest and politicization, if not suppressed, would lead to social revolution and the destruction of traditional class hierarchies, they condemned laissez-faire liberalism as inadequate to cope with either the immediate economic emergency or the complex transformations of twentieth-century society that were threatening elite control. Soon, a bitter power struggle had broken out between "liberal" and "authoritarian" elitist factions throughout the region, and by the mid 1930s, the prevailing drift in regional politics was clearly in the direction of the latter.[9]

Wherever they came to power in southeastern South America, the authoritarian factions displayed similar patterns of behavior, several of which caused their regimes to be viewed as "fascist" by world opinion. Seizure of power was inevitably followed by a suspension of civil rights and democratic processes. National legislatures were quickly closed or emasculated, the traditional political parties banned, opposition elements jailed, the courts purged, strikes outlawed, the press tightly controlled by new state censorship and propaganda agencies. Such coercive measures were justified by the need for stable and effective government and by the supremacy of the collective national interest over individual liberties. In Argentina, General Uriburu, a career army officer from the western provincial aristocracy, imprisoned civilian politicians, deported trade-union organizers, and executed several radical extremists during his short-lived dictatorship.[10] A decade later, a military coup d'état brought Juan Perón, a professional officer from the rural middle classes, to power as part of an armed-forces junta dedicated to "an inflexible dictatorship" that would make "the people . . . work, deprive themselves, and obey."[11] In Brazil, Getúlio Vargas, a professional politician from the "cattle oligarchy," initially adhered to constitutional processes, governing with a mixed coalition of liberal and authoritarian advisers. In 1937, however, facing challenges from native Brazilian communist and fascist movements and constitutionally prohibited from running for reelection, Vargas suddenly carried out an internal coup d'état orchestrated by his authoritarian supporters. Deriding "the decadence of liberal and individualistic democracy," he abolished Brazil's political parties, closed the Brazilian congress, and established a strict, authoritarian military-based dictatorship committed to "political and social peace."[12]

In addition, the region's authoritarian regimes displayed a marked predilection for corporatist administrative structures. The corporate state offered them a seemingly efficacious mechanism with which to co-opt the appeal of Marxist agitators and preempt growing lower-class unrest. By granting restive workers and peasants functional representation in governmental structures, the lower classes could be given the illusion of greater participation in national decision-making and their interest groups assimilated within the traditional hierarchical, elite-controlled system. Uriburu, for example, attempted to reform Argentina's constitution in the direction of functional legislative representation.[13] Vargas, after turning to dictatorship, immediately promulgated a new constitution establishing a corporate state in Brazil—the *Estado novo* ("new state"), modeled on Salazar's corporatist *Estado novo* in Portugal. Drafted by Francisco Campos, an authoritarian ideologue who believed that "corporatism kills communism just as liberalism breeds [it]," the new constitution provided Vargas with a corporative National Economic Council of business, professional, and labor advisers.[14] Although Perón avoided overtly corporatist forms, probably due to the increasingly unfavorable international atmosphere of the mid 1940s, his widely publicized Justicialist social philosophy, his consolidation of Argentina's urban workers into a single government-controlled labor syndicate, and his efforts to eliminate the country's national association of manufacturers (the Unión Industrial Argentina) in favor of a state-controlled syndicate of industrialists were inherently corporatist conceptualizations.[15]

Wherever they came to power, the region's authoritarian factions also massively expanded the powers and responsibilities of the state in both the social and economic spheres. Traditional laissez-faire states—already in partial decline with the appearance of early entities of state economic intervention in the region (coffee subsidization in Brazil, creation of a national petroleum agency in Argentina and of the first state-owned industrial enterprises in Uruguay)—gave way to actively interventionist states committed to far-reaching, if nevertheless essentially defensive, programs of national modernization. In the social sphere, paternalistic state welfare programs were inaugurated in order to provide a rudimentary level of social security, medical care, education, and public housing that would further deflate revolutionary social pressures and appease the lower classes, keeping them quiescent and submissive within the existing social structure. At the same time, however, programs of fundamental land reform or income redistribution were consistently avoided. And if some authoritarian leaders—Uriburu in Argentina, for example, like his Iberian counterparts Salazar in Portugal and Franco in Spain—manifested a total disdain for mass-based support, others did not fail to appreciate the tremendous political power and popular support that could be harnessed by social-welfare measures and populist rhetoric. Indeed, something of a "right-left" continuum is discernible among the region's authoritarian regimes, with a "reactionary" subtype at one end of their political spectrum and a "progressive reformist" variant at the other. While Uriburu, for example, did little to conceal his contempt for the "illiterate masses,"[16] Vargas's educational and labor reforms (pensions, minimum-wage laws, unemployment compensation, paid vacations, etc.) earned him the loyal support of Brazil's urban trade unions,[17] and Perón spoke so zealously of the need for social reform and granted so many employment benefits to urban workers that some observers—including the Argentine lower classes—believed that he was conducting a veritable social revolution. "The conservative classes," Perón later recalled, had "lost their instinct of self-preservation. Their unrestricted ambitions to keep everything for themselves, their purpose of never sharing the advantages accumulated, blinded them to the evidence: whoever wishes to keep everything will lose everything. They did not understand that their adjustment to the tremendous changes suffered by the world was a question of life and death. The truly conservative thing to be was, precisely, to be revolutionary. But they did not understand this!"[18]

It was in the economic sphere, however, that southeastern South America's authoritarian regimes expanded the role of the state most significantly. Outraged by past economic policies that had left their nations helpless against the onslaught of the world depression, the authoritarian factions bitterly denounced the liberal elites as a corrupt and irresponsible *vendepatria* oligarchy (an oligarchy of "country-sellers"), accusing them of deliberately condemning their nations to economic underdevelopment and a position of inferiority in world affairs in return for personal financial gain. Unrestricted free trade, they charged, had transformed their countries into subservient neocolonial dependencies of the leading industrial powers, while laissez-faire, open-door policies had merely enabled foreign capital to control and exploit sovereign national resources. To remedy such conditions, authoritarian leaders invariably turned to nationalistic state controls, moving rapidly toward the creation of mixed state-capitalist economies. Nationalistic state-directed programs of economic development were launched in an effort to achieve national economic independence from foreign capital and foreign markets. Key sectors of the private economy—notably transportation, communications, public utilities, and mineral resources—were nationalized and placed under state control. State-directed industrial-development projects and import-substitution programs attempted to diversify the national economy and emancipate it from its tradition of vulnerable dependence on export agriculture, foreign manufactured goods, and international trade. Vargas and Perón, for example, each heralded the construction of a domestic steel plant as a symbol of national economic independence from the industrial powers. Discriminatory trade practices and nationalistic commercial mechanisms, similar to those employed by Europe's fascist states, were inevitably adopted in the drive for industrial self-sufficiency. Exchange controls and

22

import quotas, for example, were utilized by authoritarian regimes throughout the region to channel international-exchange earnings and investment capital into government-designated development programs. Uriburu, Vargas, and Perón each raised tariff barriers to protect developing infant industries, while Perón and Paraguay's Morínigo experimented with monopolistic state trading agencies. Finally, restrictive state regulatory controls were placed over foreign investors and foreign enterprises in an effort to close the open door to exploitative foreign capital. Vargas, Perón, and Morínigo not only imposed stiff taxes on foreign capital and tightly regulated its operations in their nations but expropriated selected foreign-owned corporations as well.[19]

Emerging as the predominant political force in southeastern South America during the 1930s, these "authoritarian nationalist" dictatorships, with their nationalistic, statist, and autarkic approach to economic development, their sensitivity to economic exploitation by the industrial nations, and their antagonism toward international free trade, presented a major obstacle to the Roosevelt administration's plans to develop new trade links and new markets for United States industrial exports in the region.

3

Great-Power Rivalry in
Southeastern South America,
1933–41

Before it could expect to develop closer trade relations with the nations of southeastern South America, the United States first had to improve its reputation in the region. Since attaining the status of a major world power in the last years of the nineteenth century, the United States had been aggressively extending its power southward in the hemisphere, converting the Caribbean basin into a United States sphere of influence with a flood of private investment capital, a tightening control over that region's foreign commerce, and a heavy-handed use of military power to enforce political and fiscal stability and defend United States interests in the Caribbean from European competitors. Direct United States military interventions had been limited to this contiguous north-ernmost tier of Latin America, generally paralleling United States trade and investments in the hemisphere—which were concentrated in Mexico, Central America, Cuba, and the other island nations of the Caribbean and decreased in a descending scale southward to their point of least significance in southeastern South America.[1] Nevertheless, the United States record of economic expansionism and arbitrary interventions in the Caribbean basin had, by the 1930s, spread a legacy of resentment and distrust throughout South America.

An imperialistic image was scarcely conducive to an expansion of United States export markets in Latin America, and the Roosevelt administration lost no time in publicly renouncing the use of force and dedicating the United States to behavior more befitting a "good neighbor" in the hemisphere community. At the Seventh Inter-American Conference of American States at Montevideo, Uruguay, in December 1933, Secretary of State Cordell Hull, the chief architect of the administration's reciprocal trade agreements program, worked energetically to allay Latin American hostility, pledging that "no government need fear

25

any intervention on the part of the United States under the Roosevelt administration" and signing a conference declaration that "no state has the right to intervene in the internal or external affairs of another." In return, Hull secured a resolution that endorsed "liberalization of international economic relations," "substantial reductions of basic trade barriers and liberalization of commercial policy, . . . elimination of those duties and restrictions which retard most severely the normal flow of international trade," and commercial agreements based on "the most-favored-nation clause in its unconditional and unrestricted form." The result, he reported confidentially to Roosevelt, would be "an increase of production and trade for the United States."[2]

An ensuing United States drive to overcome British commercial supremacy in southeastern South America by negotiating reciprocal trade agreements and promoting United States industrial exports met with only partial success, however. The primary impediment was a basic lack of complementarity between the economies of the two areas. Most of the leading export products of southeastern South America—meats, grains, cotton—competed with United States agricultural exports in world markets, in contrast to the complementary relationship that linked the region's commerce to the food-importing industrial economies of Europe.[3] Lacking markets in the United States for their exports, the nations of southeastern South America had little interest in trade agreements with the Roosevelt administration, and the State Department was able to negotiate only one reciprocal trade agreement in the region during the 1930s—a 1935 accord with Brazil permitting Brazilian coffee and cacao to enter the United States duty-free in return for Brazilian tariff reductions on United States automobiles, motorcycles, refrigerators, and radios. And this agreement Cordell Hull secured only after first threatening to increase United States tariff rates on imports of Brazilian coffee.[4]

No such lack of complementarity obstructed German economic initiatives in southeastern South America. Like Great Britain a heavy importer of raw materials, Germany looked upon the region not only as an attractive export market for its industrial commodities but as a source of supply for both foodstuffs and the raw materials needed to fuel German industrial expansion—the cotton for its textile mills, the bauxite for its developing aluminum industry, and the iron ore and manganese for its steel production. Accordingly, Hitler launched an aggressive state-directed trade assault on southeastern South America, working closely with German industrialists in a carefully coordinated drive to promote German commerce and ruthlessly undercut British and United States economic competition. Sales representatives of private

German firms flooded the region, coordinating their activities with German diplomatic staffs and aided by government subsidies for their manufactured goods which enabled them to undersell competitive British and United States exports so effectively that United States businessmen were soon complaining to the State Department about unfair competition. At the same time, official German trade missions headed by representatives of the state bank and the ministries of foreign affairs, economics, and agriculture toured the region, offering attractive prices for raw materials, promoting sales of German industrial goods, and playing adroitly on the region's industrial aspirations by pledging German financial and technical assistance for industrial development projects. As a result, Germany successfully negotiated bilateral trade agreements with Argentina, Brazil, and Uruguay—each of which was based on a cleverly devised barter system by which Germany paid for purchases of raw materials, not with hard currency that could be spent in other industrial markets, but with discounted compensation marks that could be used only for purchases of German products. To the nations of southeastern South America, lured by the lucrative new German export market and seductively discounted German manufactured goods, such an arrangement was not unattractive. Nevertheless, with each new German raw-materials purchase increasing southeastern South America's reliance on German industrial exports, bilateral barter trade pointed to an eventual German monopoly over the region's trade to the complete exclusion of other industrial nations, precluding the open system of multilateral free trade envisioned by the Roosevelt administration in its reciprocal trade agreements program, and as a consequence each German barter agreement quickly drew angry United States protests and charges of trade discrimination.[5]

As a result of its aggressive trade tactics, Germany's economic influence in southeastern South America expanded dramatically between 1933 and 1938. During that period, Germany increased the total volume of its trade with the region by 137 percent, as compared to gains of 41 percent by the United States and 19 percent by Great Britain. At the same time, Germany's relative share of the region's foreign trade increased from less than 10 percent in 1933 to almost 16 percent in 1938, while Great Britain's share of the region's trade was decreasing from 23 percent to less than 20, and the United States' share was also declining slightly, from 18.9 percent to 18.7 percent (see table 1).

German purchases of southeastern South America's export products rose by 136 percent between 1933 and 1938, while British purchases were increasing by 13 percent and those of the United States by only 4 percent. Great Britain continued to be the region's principal customer, but its

TABLE 1

Trade between Nations of Southeastern South America and Great Britain, Germany, and the United States, 1933 and 1938

	Year	Total Trade (In Millions)	Trade with Great Britain		Trade with Germany		Trade with the United States	
			In Millions	% of Total Trade	In Millions	% of Total Trade	In Millions	% of Total Trade
Argentina	1933*	$ 624.108	$186.596	29.9	$ 56.658	9.1	$ 62.276	10.0
	1938	837.398	220.145	26.3	91.907	11.0	109.289	13.1
Brazil	1933*	392.989	49.688	12.6	38.626	9.8	139.202	35.4
	1938	590.882	56.541	9.6	130.224	22.0	173.028	29.3
Paraguay	1933*	11.895	.460	3.9	.225	1.9	.377	3.2
	1938	14.550	1.637	11.3	1.858	12.8	1.578	10.8
Uruguay	1933*	76.801	20.587	26.8	9.244	12.0	6.745	8.8
	1938	123.227	28.707	23.3	24.482	19.9	9.647	7.8
Region	1933*	1,105.793	257.331	23.3	104.753	9.5	208.600	18.9
	1938	1,566.057	307.030	19.6	248.471	15.9	293.542	18.7

SOURCES: United States, Department of Commerce, *Foreign Commerce Yearbook, 1936* (Washington, D.C.: Government Printing Office, 1937), pp. 184, 189, 198, 199, 252–53, 265, 267; ibid., *1948* (Washington, D.C.: Government Printing Office, 1950), pp. 291, 383, 404; and ibid., *1949* (Washington, D.C.: Government Printing Office, 1951), p. 268.

* Dollar values for 1933 are estimates, because the violent fluctuation in the values of international currencies during 1933 made precise dollar conversions of foreign-trade figures impossible. Percentage figures for 1933, however, are precise, since they were based on the respective South American currencies rather than converted dollar values.

TABLE 2

Exports from Nations of Southeastern South America to Great Britain, Germany, and the United States, 1933 and 1938

From	Year	Total Exports In Millions	Exports to Great Britain In Millions	% of Total Exports	Exports to Germany In Millions	% of Total Exports	Exports to the United States In Millions	% of Total Exports
Argentina	1933*	$346.645	$127.219	36.7	$ 26.692	7.7	$ 27.038	7.8
	1938	409.212	134.265	32.8	47.788	11.7	34.641	8.5
Brazil	1933*	223.127	16.735	7.5	18.073	8.1	103.531	46.4
	1938	295.558	25.915	8.8	56.348	19.1	101.458	34.3
Paraguay	1933*	6.864	.003	0.0	.035	0.5	.112	1.6
	1938	6.966	.907	13.0	.991	14.2	.852	12.2
Uruguay	1933*	40.209	13.269	33.0	5.951	14.8	3.378	8.4
	1938	61.660	16.133	26.2	14.490	23.5	2.449	4.0
Region	1933*	616.845	157.226	25.5	50.751	8.2	134.059	21.7
	1938	773.396	177.220	22.9	119.617	15.5	139.400	18.0

Sources: United States, Department of Commerce, *Foreign Commerce Yearbook, 1936* (Washington, D.C.: Government Printing Office, 1937), pp. 184, 189, 198, 199, 252–53, 265, 267; ibid., *1948* (Washington, D.C.: Government Printing Office, 1950), pp. 291, 383, 404; and ibid., *1949* (Washington, D.C.: Government Printing Office, 1951), p. 268.

* Dollar values for 1933 are estimates, because the violent fluctuation in the values of international currencies during 1933 made precise dollar conversions of foreign-trade figures impossible. Percentage figures for 1933, however, are precise, since they were based on the respective South American currencies rather than converted dollar values.

relative share of the region's export trade declined from 26 percent to less than 23 percent between 1933 and 1938, during which time the United States' share also decreased, from 22 percent to 18 percent, while Germany's share almost doubled, from 8 percent to nearly 16 (see table 2). By 1938, Germany was out-purchasing the United States in Argentina, Paraguay, and Uruguay.

Germany's position as a supplier of southeastern South America's manufactured imports also improved markedly. German sales to the region increased by 139 percent between 1933 and 1938, as compared to increases of 107 percent by the United States and 30 percent by Great Britain. The United States edged ahead of Great Britain as the region's leading supplier of industrial goods, increasing its relative share of the region's imports from 15 percent in 1933 to 19 percent in 1938, as the British portion dropped from 21 percent to nearly 16; but Germany's share grew from 11 percent to over 16 percent during the same period, moving Germany from a distant third place into a position of equal strength with Great Britain and close behind the United States (see table 3). Indeed, by 1938, Germany had become the principal source of industrial goods for Brazil and Paraguay and was out-selling the United States in Uruguay as well, as German exporters aggressively carved out leading positions in the marketing of electrical supplies, chemicals and pharmaceuticals, railway equipment, agricultural machinery, armaments, household utensils, and precision medical and photographic instruments. At the same time, German commercial firms—construction companies, hardware retailers, commercial airlines, banks, insurance companies, hotels, news wire-services—were penetrating the region in ever-increasing numbers.[6]

By 1938, then, Germany had emerged as a major economic power in southeastern South America and, based on 1933–38 rates of trade expansion, was threatening to soon outdistance the United States in the race to replace Great Britain as the region's dominant industrial trading partner.

Beginning in 1938, however, Hitler committed Germany to a policy of territorial expansion in Europe, and for the next three years, as Germany and the United States drifted from economic competition toward direct military confrontation, their commercial rivalry in southeastern South America intensified sharply, taking on new strategic geopolitical implications. A key factor in Hitler's turn to military aggression was his determination to achieve economic autarky. The acquisition of a territorial empire was a logical extension of the drive for total economic self-sufficiency in nations lacking the raw materials needed for industrialization, and in 1936, Germany, Italy, and Japan—

TABLE 3

IMPORTS BY NATIONS OF SOUTHEASTERN SOUTH AMERICA
FROM GREAT BRITAIN, GERMANY, AND THE UNITED STATES, 1933 AND 1938

To	Year	TOTAL IMPORTS In Millions	IMPORTS FROM GREAT BRITAIN In Millions	% of Total Imports	IMPORTS FROM GERMANY In Millions	% of Total Imports	IMPORTS FROM THE UNITED STATES In Millions	% of Total Imports
Argentina	1933*	$277.463	$ 59.377	21.4	$ 29.966	10.8	$ 35.238	12.7
	1938	428.186	85.880	20.1	44.119	10.3	74.648	17.4
Brazil	1933*	169.862	32.953	19.4	20.553	12.1	35.671	21.0
	1938	295.324	30.626	10.4	73.876	25.0	71.570	24.2
Paraguay	1933*	5.031	.457	9.1	.190	3.8	.265	5.3
	1938	7.584	.730	9.6	.867	11.4	.726	9.6
Uruguay	1933*	36.592	7.318	20.0	3.293	9.0	3.367	9.2
	1938	61.567	12.574	20.4	9.992	16.2	7.198	11.7
Region	1933*	488.948	100.105	20.5	54.002	11.0	74.541	15.2
	1938	792.661	129.810	16.4	128.854	16.3	154.142	19.4

SOURCES: United States, Department of Commerce, *Foreign Commerce Yearbook, 1936* (Washington, D.C.: Government Printing Office, 1937), pp. 184, 189, 198, 199, 252–53, 265, 267; ibid., *1948* (Washington, D.C.: Government Printing Office, 1950), pp. 291, 383, 404; and ibid., *1949* (Washington, D.C.: Government Printing Office, 1951), p. 268.

* Dollar values for 1933 are estimates, because the violent fluctuation in the values of international currencies during 1933 made precise dollar conversions of foreign-trade figures impossible. Percentage figures for 1933, however, are precise, since they were based on the respective South American currencies rather than converted dollar values.

the three rising industrial powers without adequate domestic supplies of oil, iron ore, and the other natural resources essential to heavy industry—joined together in pacts of mutual support for their respective efforts to carve out empires in Europe, Africa, and Asia.[7] Hitler had already reoccupied Germany's coal-rich Saar basin, which had been annexed by France as part of the World War I peace settlement, and in 1938, he moved to forge a German-controlled commonwealth in central Europe, annexing Austria and much of Czechoslovakia. When Poland rejected his territorial demands, Hitler responded with a military invasion in September 1939, igniting full-scale war against Poland's allies, Great Britain and France. By June of 1940, German forces had overrun most of western Europe, prompting Mussolini to opportunistically bring Italy into the war as Germany's ally. When a German air assault against Great Britain stalemated, Hitler redirected his efforts toward the consolidation of German hegemony in eastern Europe, invading the Soviet Union in June 1941.

As Hitler's armies marched victoriously across continental Europe, the British navy swept German merchant shipping from the Atlantic sea lanes, severing German trade links with Latin America. To preserve Germany's hard-earned economic influence in southeastern South America, Hitler's diplomatic representatives confidently assured the region's governmental and business leaders that a quick and decisive German military victory in the European war was inevitable, emphasizing that since Europe's total import and export trade would soon be under German control, those nations of southeastern South America that wished to maintain their European markets would be well advised to immediately strengthen their commercial ties with Germany. Those nations that failed to do so, the Germans hinted, could expect German economic retaliation after the war. Meanwhile, sales representatives of private German firms were working strenuously to maintain their position in the region's import markets, confidently guaranteeing local customers quick delivery of German merchandise and even agreeing to pay fines in the event that stipulated delivery dates were not met.[8]

Simultaneously, Germany endeavored to win political support from the nations of the region. Propaganda pamphlets and German-subsidized local newspapers cultivated sympathy for the Third Reich in public opinion, decrying "decadent democracy" and "Anglo-Saxon economic imperialism," stressing the justice of German war aims, and lauding fascism as the most effective path to national progress among "virile" nations. German embassies assiduously cultivated local authoritarian nationalists with lavish social gatherings and with financial assistance for their political machinations against local liberal elements. Taking advantage of the prominent role that German military missions had traditionally played in the training of the region's armed forces, the Germans concentrated special attention on politically influential authoritarian nationalist military officers, promising industrialization assistance and "virtually unlimited" supplies of military equipment as soon as the war was over, and inviting officers to study in German military academies where they could observe at first hand the progress and strength achieved by Germany under fascism. Below the surface, in the meantime, German agents were establishing covert espionage networks in coastal areas to report British ship movements to German submarines.[9]

Hitler's aggressive foreign policy raised serious apprehensions within the Roosevelt administration regarding Germany's intentions in Latin America. U.S. policy-makers perceived several potential German threats to United States interests in the hemisphere, and their concern focused particularly on southeastern South America, the region of the hemisphere farthest removed from United States power and influence. United States military leaders suspected that Hitler harbored goals of world conquest and that once in unchallenged control of Europe, he intended to invade the Western Hemisphere with a military thrust through eastern South America.[10] United States officials also feared that Germany might gain political hegemony in southeastern South America without resorting to military force. German cultivation of the region's authoritarian nationalists raised suspicions in Washington that Hitler was seeking to manipulate domestic politics there to his own advantage by secretly instigating internal political revolutions that would bring pro-German puppets to power and provide Germany with a dependent bloc of client regimes in the southern part of the hemisphere. Such fears came to a head in May 1940, when, in response to British warnings that a "Nazi coup" was imminent in Uruguay and that Brazil, Argentina, and Paraguay were also dangerously vulnerable to "an internal putsch by . . . pro-German politicians," the Roosevelt administration dispatched two heavy naval cruisers to the Rio de la Plata "as a preventative step" and drew up contingency plans—designated Pot of Gold—for the airlifting of ten thousand United States troops to Brazil.[11] In addition, the United States was equally concerned that if Great Britain and its navy were defeated, the resulting preponderance of German power in Europe and the Atlantic would prompt many South American nations to willingly align themselves in the German orbit for the sake of expediency. "In the event of a British defeat," a January 1941 administration study concluded, "only the moral, and the armed, strength of the United States" would prevent the "dominant class" of southern South

America "from adopting an appeasement policy."[12] Finally, administration officials were alarmed over the possibility that German economic expansionism might effectively block the United States' own expansionist aims in Latin America and other areas of the globe, eventually reducing the United States to the status of a second-rate power in world affairs. Hitler, the United States embassy in Berlin had predicted, "will not attack the Americans by force, as he can attain his aims by other methods, once he has established his domination over the countries of Europe. He will strangle the United States economically and financially and . . . confront the United States within a brief measure of time with the impossible tasks of adjusting its system to an economy in which it will be excluded from access to all foreign markets."[13] Trade trends in South America between 1933 and 1938 seemed to portend just such a contingency. If German military conquests in Europe added the Latin American trade of Great Britain, France, and the smaller countries of continental Europe to Germany's already substantial share of Latin American imports and exports, a 1941 administration analysis warned, "German-controlled European trade would far exceed that of the United States," creating "a tremendous obstacle to United States trade with Latin America" and seriously jeopardizing "the economic position of the United States in the other American republics."[14]

Contributing heavily to the Roosevelt administration's fears was the presence in Latin America of a potential fifth column of some 1.5 million German immigrants.[15] Again, United States concern centered primarily on southeastern South America, where nearly one million of the German immigrants were concentrated. Many had left Germany in the catastrophic years following World War I, resettling in the remote upper reaches of the Rio de la Plata basin, where the southernmost Brazilian states of Paraná, Santa Catarina, and Rio Grande do Sul, Argentina's Misiones and Corrientes provinces, and the adjacent border region of southeastern Paraguay converge.[16] There they had established prosperous agricultural colonies, winning local respect and admiration for their hard work and industriousness and consolidating positions of influence in the economies of their host countries. For the most part, the German immigrants had remained unassimilated and aloof in their new surroundings, maintaining their ethnic identity in dress and customs, continuing to speak only German, and independently operating their own German-language schools, churches, and cultural societies. In the late 1920s, representatives of Hitler's National Socialist movement arrived from Germany to begin proselytizing among the immigrant colonies, where they evoked an enthusiastic response from the many immigrants who had fled the ruin of postwar Germany but who still retained strong feelings of national loyalty and a desire to see Germany's national power and honor restored. After 1933, Hitler's government devoted considerable attention to increasing its control over the immigrants. Hitler's agents organized local National Socialist movements in each community, usually under the direction of National Socialist schoolmasters sent from Germany to infiltrate the immigrants' school systems. Where necessary, terrorist methods were employed to eliminate obstinately anti-Nazi community leaders. At the same time, German-language newspapers subsidized by German embassies circulated among the immigrants, playing upon nationalist sentiments and providing glowing reports of life in Hitler's "new Germany." The popularity of National Socialism increased noticeably among the immigrant communities during the late 1930s as Hitler achieved his succession of impressive diplomatic and military triumphs in Europe, and by the end of the decade, local German schools in Argentina, Brazil, and Paraguay were openly displaying Nazi swastikas and portraits of Hitler.[17] By 1940, according to alarmed United States officials, Argentina's Misiones Province had been "virtually turned into a Nazi state."[18] Hitler's growing control over the German immigrants initially prompted U.S. fears that they would be used to exert pressure and influence on the governments of southeastern South America on behalf of German political and economic penetration. The discovery in 1940 of weapons caches among pro-Nazi Germans in Argentina and Uruguay, however, raised the more dangerous possibility that the immigrants were being equipped for a paramilitary role in domestic coups or in support of a German invasion of the Americas.[19]

In 1938, the Roosevelt administration began a diplomatic counteroffensive designed to thwart further German expansion in the Western Hemisphere by bringing all of Latin America within the political and economic orbit of the United States. At the Eighth International Conference of American States at Lima in December 1938 and at subsequent hemispheric conferences at Panama in 1939 and Havana in 1940, United States delegations vigorously sought to convince their Latin American counterparts of the dangers of German imperialism and of the urgent need for "continental solidarity" and a United States–Latin American security pact against European aggression, simultaneously proposing increased commercial and economic cooperation among the American republics based on "liberal principles of international trade."[20] The State Department, in 1938, began to actively cultivate pro–United States sentiments and support for the democratic free-enterprise system in Latin American public opinion, establishing a Division of Cultural Relations to initiate cultural-exchange programs and an Interdepartmental Committee on Cooperation with the American Republics to develop an effective propaganda campaign.[21] Roosevelt lent his personal assistance to such efforts by making public speeches that warned of ominous Nazi designs on the Americas, going so far on one occasion as to use a fraudulent "secret map" to "prove" that Hitler planned to divide South America into "five vassal states."[22]

In addition, the administration promoted closer military cooperation between the United States and Latin America. Representatives of the departments of State, War, and Navy formed a standing liaison committee in January 1938 to coordinate hemispheric defense strategy, and foremost among their recommendations was the need to increase United States influence among Latin America's armed forces. Accordingly, a United States military-mission program was inaugurated in 1938, designed to oust German missions from their influential positions in the training of Latin American armed forces by underbidding them in the cost of professional instruction. The United States similarly began to compete with Germany by inviting large numbers of Latin American officers to study in United States military schools and by offering obsolete and surplus military equipment to the Latin Americans at cost. In return, the administration requested air- and naval-base rights in Latin America for U.S. military forces in preparation for possible hemispheric defense operations.[23]

The central thrust of the United States counteroffensive, however, was a program of financial and technical assistance for Latin American economic development—the first foreign-aid program in United States history. To counter German economic influence in the hemisphere and at the same time to surmount the rising tide of Latin American economic nationalism which posed an equally serious obstacle to United States economic expansion, the Roosevelt administration again borrowed a German tactic, playing on the Latin Americans' aspirations for development by offering to assist them in programs of industrial development. In offering assistance, United States officials first urged the Latin Americans to rely primarily on private investment and foreign capital to develop their economies. Stressing the impressive results that laissez-faire capitalism and an open door for private British investment capital had produced in the United States' great industrial revolution of the nineteenth century (but conveniently ignoring the important role that high protective tariffs had played in U.S. industrial development), United States officials consistently pressed the Latin Americans to adopt a similar model in their own development programs, encouraging them to allow U.S. private enterprise and U.S. investment capital to provide their economies with modern manufacturing infrastructures and discouraging all nationalistic state-directed approaches to industrial development that involved restrictions on private enterprise and foreign investment. Where Latin American nationalism proved unyielding, however, or where private U.S. capital found investment opportunities unenticing, the Roosevelt administration plowed United States public funds into Latin American development projects.[24]

In 1938, the Export-Import Bank granted its first low-interest development loans to Latin American governments. At the September 1939 Panama Conference, as German armies absorbed Poland, the Roosevelt administration announced its eagerness to cooperate in Latin America's development, and subsequently took the lead in organizing an Inter-American Development Commission to plan cooperative development projects. To finance such undertakings the United States, in 1940, raised the lending authority of the Export-Import Bank from $200 million to $700 million, timing the increase to coincide with the Havana Conference in order to provide added bargaining power for the U.S. delegation in its efforts to promote hemispheric solidarity after the fall of France.[25] Simultaneously, Nelson Rockefeller's new Office of the Coordinator of Inter-American Affairs launched a series of cooperative programs designed to win friends in the hemisphere—providing free agricultural training programs, public-health programs, and a technical assistance program that made U.S. budgetary and monetary experts available to Latin American governments to assist them in modernizing their bureaucracies and financial institutions along United States patterns.

United States development aid invariably tied the recipient to a closer relationship with U.S. private enterprise. The Export-Import Bank, for example, required that its loans be used "to finance the purchase of materials and equipment manufactured in the United States" and that those materials be shipped to the purchaser in United States vessels.[26] The bank also aggressively promoted the use of U.S. engineers and construction companies in all development projects for which it loaned funds. Such stipulations, a United States official observed, in effect made Export-Import Bank development loans indirect government subsidies to private U.S. firms, "helping exporters to meet subsidized competition of Germany in South America."[27] The bank also made careful distinctions in the types of industrialization projects which it funded, favoring proposals for raw-materials processing plants and light consumer-goods industries that would continue to require large imports of U.S. tools, machinery, and parts, and reserving assistance in the development of the heavy capital-goods industries essential for industrial self-sufficiency—steel, cement, electric power, and so forth—to those Latin American nations whose friendship was deemed vital to United States interests. The Inter-American Development Commission, with

Nelson Rockefeller and other United States officials as its executive directors, tended to stress Latin American responsibilities in guaranteeing fair treatment and protection to United States investment capital and looked with disfavor on development proposals that were not advantageous to United States commerce.[28] And after the Roosevelt administration, in July 1941, issued a "proclaimed list" of anti-American firms in the hemisphere alleged to be controlled by Germany and its allies and with which United States citizens were forbidden to trade, it occasionally used development aid as a reward for Latin American governments that honored the list and transferred their commercial dealings from "proclaimed" enterprises to United States firms.

Throughout this period of United States–German rivalry, the governments of southeastern South America invariably tended to define their national interests in world affairs in terms of economic expediency. With a consistency that clearly presaged the emergence of a north-south realignment of global power configurations during the 1970s, policy-formulators throughout the region viewed the international power struggles of the late 1930s as essentially reflecting the rival imperialisms of the leading Northern Hemisphere industrial nations as they competed for global spheres of influence. Based on their own historical experiences, the United States' Office of Strategic Services reported, the nations of the region tended to "look upon all strong powers as potential dangers" and had reason to fear "domination by Anglo-American interests as much as, if not more than," Nazi domination.[29] As a result, the region's leaders were suspicious of United States efforts to portray Germany as the major threat to their sovereignty, and they remained largely unresponsive to the Roosevelt administration's appeals for hemispheric unity against potential German aggression. When, for example, the United States delegation to the 1938 Lima Conference proposed a hemispheric collective-security pact against outside aggression, Argentina, Paraguay, and Uruguay refused to join in any hostile references to Germany and instead pointedly suggested that the United States proposal be expanded to encompass threats from either a "continental or extracontinental power."[30] Instead of hemispheric solidarity with one of the competing industrial powers, the region's leaders tended to favor a neutral nonalignment as their safest and wisest course, at least until it became clearer which Northern Hemisphere nation was ultimately to prevail in world affairs. The central question "constantly in the minds of the statesmen and leaders here," the United States legation in Paraguay reported, is "whether greater prosperity and comfort for each nation will result from a German world-control or an Anglo-Franco-American system. . . . From their standpoint it is common prudence to favor and conciliate those powers which will hold a predominant place in the future."[31]

A variety of practical considerations counseled the nations of the region to adopt a posture of nonalignment. Foremost was the need to safeguard their fragile economies by maintaining friendly trade relations with all of the competing industrial powers. The interruption of commercial shipping between Europe and the Western Hemisphere that followed the outbreak of naval warfare in the Atlantic in 1939 automatically increased their reliance on United States markets, a reliance which, the region's leaders recognized, would of necessity persist for the duration of the war in Europe. Yet at the same time, the distinct possibility, by mid 1940, that Germany might soon control the entire European economy made it essential for nations whose export sales were traditionally oriented toward European markets to remain on good terms with Hitler's government.[32]

Domestic political considerations also disposed the region's governments to avoid a hemispheric alliance hostile to Germany and her ally, Italy. Since the mid nineteenth century, those two nations had furnished a major proportion of southeastern South America's large inflow of immigrants, and by the 1930s, persons of German and Italian descent constituted a significant element in the region's population and exerted a heavy influence on the political and economic life of each nation. Argentina, its delegation to the Lima Conference informed the United States, was unwilling to offend the very nations which "give lifeblood to our nation and buy our products."[33] In addition, the balance of power in each nation's domestic politics guaranteed that any definitive international alignment by an incumbent regime would generate controversy and instability. The region's liberal elites generally tended to be sympathetic toward the "democracies," having close economic ties with British capital, and respecting the potential economic and military might of the United States should the "Colossus of the North" choose to deploy its full power in South America. On the other hand, the forces of authoritarian nationalism constituted a powerful domestic lobby against solidarity with the United States or Great Britain. Sharing a vague ideological kinship with European fascism, they were deeply impressed by the strength and stability that had been achieved in Germany and Italy under corporatist dictatorships. They also derived a large measure of satisfaction in seeing the very symbol of European liberalism and great-power exploitation in their region—Great Britain—brought to her knees by the forces of European totalitarian nationalism; nor was the ideological significance of the 1941 German invasion of the Soviet Union —the headquarters of the international movement for social revolution— lost upon them.[34] In particular, the region's armed forces—traditional centers of political influence and authoritarian nationalist sentiment— were impressed by the power and efficiency of the German armed forces as they swept across Europe, believing that such an awesome and seem- ingly invincible force guaranteed an early German victory in the Euro- pean war. According to a 1941 intelligence analysis produced by the United States Office of Strategic Services, for example, although the politically powerful Brazilian army was "the chief focus in Brazil of sentiment adverse to close cooperation with the United States," it was "not convinced that a victorious Germany would constitute a menace to Brazil." "Many of the officers," the O.S.S. concluded, "have lived in Germany . . . , have had training in German army schools," and "look almost with reverence at the Nazi military machine; to them the totalitarian forms of government are far more acceptable than the forms of a liberal democracy."[35]

A final incentive for nonalignment was the unprecedented oppor- tunity that the escalating international power struggle provided the region's governments to secure economic assistance. By playing the United States and Germany off against each other as they competed to outbid one another in attracting southeastern South America into their respective orbits, the ruling elites of the region could reap a veritable bonanza of foreign aid for industrial development and the paternalistic social-welfare programs needed to keep their lower classes quiescent within the traditional social system.[36] Of the region's leaders, none proved more adept at profiting from nonalignment than Getúlio Vargas in Brazil. Throughout the mid 1930s, Vargas maintained a carefully balanced cordiality in his relations with Germany and the United States as the two powers courted Brazil; he concluded trade agreements with each in 1935, enlisted assistance from both the German Gestapo and the United States' Federal Bureau of Investigation in the development of his secret police, and even enrolled one of his own sons at the University of Berlin and another at Johns Hopkins University.[37] After 1938, as United States–German relations deteriorated dangerously and their courtship of Brazil intensified, Vargas shrewdly encouraged the two rivals to direct their competition toward offers of assistance in developing a Brazilian steel industry, the heart of Vargas's industrialization program. By early 1939, both the German and United States governments were expressing interest in the construction of a Brazilian steel plant. The Roosevelt administration, viewing the virtually undefended northeastern "bulge" of Brazil as the most likely target for any German invasion of the Western Hemisphere and anxious to persuade Vargas to permit United States military forces to be stationed there, initially tried to interest a private United States firm—U.S. Steel Corporation—in building a Brazilian steel plant. After preliminary surveys, however, U.S. Steel pulled out in January 1940, unwilling to undertake a project that would eliminate the company's $5 million yearly steel sales to Brazil and also suspicious of Vargas's record of nationalistic attacks on foreign investment.[38] Vargas immediately informed the State Department of his "sharp disappointment" with U.S. Steel's decision, and expressed his intention to "turn in other directions." By August 1940, reports were reaching Washington that representatives of Germany's Krupp steelworks were offering Vargas "extremely advantageous terms" on a steel plant. The Roosevelt administration immediately concluded that "failure on the part of this Government to assist the Brazilians in this matter will in all probability . . . result in the immediate acceptance by Brazil of a German offer to build the plant," thereby assuring "Germany's predominance in Brazilian economic and military life . . . for many years." Whereupon the Export-Import Bank promptly agreed to loan Vargas $20 million in government funds for the construction of a modern steel plant at Volta Redonda.[39] Six years later, augmented by an additional $25 million in United States credits, Brazil possessed the largest steel complex in Latin America.

As long, then, as the United States and Germany remained willing to engage in peaceful competitive bidding for the affections of southeastern South America, it behooved the nations of the region to accept largesse from both powers without committing themselves unequivocally to either. Whether such a policy would continue to be expedient after 7 December 1941, when the United States suddenly found itself at war with Germany and its allies and immediately attempted to force a commitment of total support from each nation of the hemisphere, remained to be determined.

4

Good Neighbor in Paraguay:
José Félix Estigarribia
and the United States

No nation in the Western Hemisphere had a more firmly rooted authoritarian political tradition than Paraguay. Some three centuries of Spanish colonialism had conditioned the Paraguayans to arbitrary rule, and after attaining independence in 1811, they unhesitantly institutionalized a system of national dictatorship in the conviction that only a "strong state" could protect Paraguay from absorption by its expansionistic neighbors, Argentina and Brazil. During the ensuing half-century of national formation, three repressive "presidents-for-life"— José Gaspar Rodríguez de Francia (1814–40), Carlos Antonio López (1840–62), and Francisco Solano López (1862–70)—steadily built up Paraguay's national power, transforming the small nation into a virtual garrison state with the largest military establishment in the Rio de la Plata basin.[1]

For five decades, Paraguay's dictators imposed a stifling political stability and a primitive economic self-reliance on their new nation, preserving its independence from the hegemonic pretensions of its powerful neighbors and shielding it from the political anarchy, fiscal bankruptcy, and foreign economic domination so characteristic of other Spanish American republics during the first half of the nineteenth century. Jailings, deportations, and executions enforced absolute internal order and discipline among upper-class landowners and peasantry alike. A remarkably self-contained, state-directed economy safeguarded the land-locked nation from economic strangulation by Argentina, whose naval blockades of the Paraná River periodically closed Paraguay off from its sole outlet to the Atlantic and world commerce. To ensure sufficient surpluses of the country's principal products—wheat, tobacco, *yerba maté* tea, cotton, timber, meat, and hides—the state expropriated nearly all agricultural land, placed it in the public domain, and leased

43

it out to private cultivators under centralized state management. An extensive system of state ranches supplied the nation with horses, cattle, and mules and produced food for the army and the destitute.[2] In addition, the state monopolized the marketing of agricultural exports and plowed the resulting foreign-exchange earnings into internal modernization projects that brought modern technology into the country. State-owned processing industries (textiles, lumber, paper, leather goods) and the foundations of early heavy industry (a state-owned ironworks and an armaments facility) moved Paraguay toward a subsistence level of industrial self-sufficiency, while a state-owned railroad, state telegraph and highway systems, and a state merchant marine further augmented the nation's internal strength and self-reliance.

This period of forced growth came to an abrupt and devastating end with the War of the Triple Alliance. In 1865, Francisco Solano López led the Paraguayan people into an impossible struggle against the combined forces of Argentina, Brazil, and Uruguay, which ended only after López's death at Cerro Corá five years later. Defeat left Paraguay in ruins, its population decimated to the point of near extinction (an estimated 300,000 dead out of a population of 525,000), its crops and cattle herds and state-owned ranches destroyed, its industrial base demolished. Destroyed, too, was the authoritarian state. In 1870, the occupying armies of the victorious allies imposed an alien democratic system of government on the country under a new liberal constitution and, after stripping Paraguay of some 55,000 square miles of its territory, turned the government over to the surviving remnants of the Paraguayan elite.

After the smothering order and stability of the authoritarian state, the new "liberal state" ushered in a seventy-year era of endemic political violence and ineffectual government. Behind the empty forms of constitutional democracy, rival factions of an impoverished, dispirited oligarchy, which lacked any tradition of democratic compromise, formed two political parties and attempted to perpetuate the traditional rule-by-force. The Colorados[3] monopolized the government by means of controlled elections and stringent police powers until 1904, when they were overthrown by the Liberals, who used the same tactics to maintain themselves in power for the next three decades. In the absence of honest elections, armed revolt—by the party out of power and, more often, by dissident factions within the incumbent party as well—quickly established itself as the only effective method of transferring power, setting in motion a bewildering cycle of instability which produced no fewer than thirty-seven presidents between 1870 and 1940, only five of whom managed to complete a full term in office and not one of whom peacefully surrendered power to the opposition in a democratic election.

In its economic provisions, the constitution of 1870 rejected the state ownership and centralized controls of the authoritarian state in favor of a laissez-faire private-enterprise system. Under it, the destitute postwar regimes that inherited the prostrate nation struggled to overcome an almost total lack of operating revenues. After several million dollars in foreign loans disappeared in a spree of fraud, corruption, and mismanagement,[4] Paraguay's desperate leaders turned to the one source of funds available to them: the sale of state landholdings from the vast public domain accumulated by Francia and the two Lópezes. The state, in fact, quickly became a concessionaire, auctioning off Paraguay's lands and resources to speculators and foreign extractive corporations. Argentine, British, French, and United States companies bought up huge tracts of land and constructed factories to process and export Paraguayan livestock products, timber, and *yerba maté*. One such enterprise—Carlos Casado, Ltd., an Argentine quebracho[5] company—alone acquired a 22,000-square-mile private empire constituting nearly one-seventh of Paraguay's total territory. Gradually, these foreign estates came to resemble independent fiefdoms, maintaining their own river ports, company towns, and private railroads and issuing their own currency, free from government interference. The compliant Paraguayan state cooperatively guaranteed them a cheap and docile labor force through legislation such as an 1871 "law of forced peonage" that gave estate managers legal powers of bondage over their landless peasant workers, while government police and military forces were consistently placed at the disposal of estate owners in suppressing labor unrest and quashing any attempts by the workers to organize.

Meanwhile, most other sectors of the Paraguayan economy also fell under foreign ownership. The state railroad was sold to Argentine-Brazilian interests in 1874 to meet payments due on the squandered foreign loans. The vessels of the state merchant marine were sold for the same purpose, with the result that the Argentine Mihanovich line acquired a monopoly over Paraguayan commercial shipping, charging freight rates so exorbitant that it soon cost more to ship merchandise the one thousand miles down river from Asunción to Buenos Aires than from Buenos Aires to New York or London. British, French, German, and Spanish capital gained control of Paraguay's banking and financial structure. Insurance was monopolized by British and Argentine interests. A United States corporation received a concession to construct and operate a modern port works at Asunción, while German-Argentine capital monopolized the capital's power and transit systems.

Decade after decade, foreign capital increased its hold over the once self-contained economy. By the 1930s, nineteen private companies owned more than half of the nation's land, and the failure of successive Colorado and Liberal administrations to rehabilitate domestic industry and agriculture had left Paraguay totally reliant on costly foreign imports for its manufactured goods and—a particularly bitter irony for the traditionally fertile wheat- and cattle-producing country—most of its foodstuffs, including dairy products. The national government limped along from year to year on the trickle of customs revenues earned from the exports flowing out of the foreign-owned extractive factories, while the members of Paraguay's small governing elite managed to earn modest livelihoods in the government bureaucracy and as lawyers and managers on the staffs of the foreign corporations. Meanwhile, unnoticed and unattended, the standard of living of the vast bulk of the population degenerated to levels as low as those found anywhere in the Western Hemisphere.[6]

During the early 1930s, a long-smouldering border dispute with neighboring Bolivia suddenly erupted into full-scale hostilities, plunging Paraguay into its second major international conflict in seven decades. The Chaco War of 1932–35 further drained the country's meager resources, and although the war ended in victory over Bolivia, the cost in manpower and material (36,000 dead, $125 million in expenditures) left Paraguay utterly exhausted.[7]

An intense patriotic fervor stimulated by the Chaco War proved to be the catalyst for a revolutionary new era in national politics, however, triggering in the younger generation of Paraguayans who bore the burden of fighting the war a nationalistic reaction against their country's backward condition. Stirrings of discontent had been building below the surface for several years. A clandestine Communist party had made its appearance in 1923 and was instrumental in organizing the first small Paraguayan trade unions among Asunción workers in the mid 1920s. In 1928, a group of Asunción intellectuals, led by Juan Stefanich, organized a new political association, the Liga Nacional Independiente, and launched a protest movement calling for national renovation and far-reaching social and economic reforms—a call that attracted an enthusiastic following among Paraguayan student groups. Meanwhile, dissident young "radical" factions in both the Liberal and Colorado parties were beginning to challenge the traditional policies of their conservative party elders and were calling on their organizations to recognize the need for change and take the initiative in leading Paraguay along new paths of national development. Finally, vague rumblings of political restlessness were beginning to be heard in Paraguay's armed forces. Since the War of the Triple Alliance, the Paraguayan army had been essentially a "political army" in the sense that both the Liberals and the Colorados, when in power, had made loyal party membership a prerequisite for entry into the national military academy and the officer corps. As a result, Paraguay in effect had a Colorado army until 1904 and a Liberal army thereafter. During the 1920s, however, a new generation of junior- and middle-level officers began to resent the squalid conditions in which they and their barefoot, ill-fed troops were maintained by the impoverished national government. At the same time, these younger officers were growing increasingly disgusted with the civilian politicians' unending coups and revolutions that kept the country in continual turmoil and played havoc with officers' careers. In response, they began to contemplate an independent political role for the Paraguayan armed forces.[8]

The general mobilization for war against Bolivia threw these diverse elements together in the Chaco. There they were galvanized by a common sense of outrage at the government's failure to prepare Paraguay's armed forces adequately for national defense. So lacking in equipment was the army at the start of hostilities, in fact, that Paraguayan troops frequently were forced to arm themselves with weapons captured by hand from Bolivian units, at a heavy cost in Paraguayan casualties. In addition, the few rifles on hand in Paraguayan arsenals were of such inferior quality that they often exploded upon firing (and were accordingly dubbed *mataparaguayos,* or "Paraguayan-killers," by the cynical Paraguayan soldiers), lending credence to widely circulating rumors that past defense expenditures had been diverted into the pockets of corrupt government officials. As a result, a generation of young Paraguayans serving in the Chaco believed their government to have been criminally negligent in military preparedness, a negligence which, from their perspective, had caused the needless deaths of thousands of their comrades in arms.[9]

For three years, around the campfires of the Chaco, they exchanged their ideas and grievances, their frustration with Paraguay's backwardness, their alienation from the established order. The result was the coalescence of a broad new political current dedicated to a "Paraguayan nationalist revolution" and the building of a "new Paraguay" after the war.[10] Less an organized movement than an impulse for change, it included among its heterogeneous adherents—known collectively as *revolucionarios*—representatives from all political groupings and social classes in Paraguay. Ill defined ideologically, its main unifying themes were a disgust with the performance of recent Liberal-party regimes and of post-1870 liberal institutional structures in general, combined with a conviction that a strong new interventionist state was needed to restore the national power, prosperity, and prestige that Paraguay had enjoyed prior to 1870. Fired by war-induced nationalism, the *revolucionarios* looked longingly back to the era of the early dictators and their stable, self-sufficient authoritarian state as a veritable golden age of effective government, political tranquility, economic integrity, and national glory, while by comparison, the subsequent experience with liberal institutions seemed synonymous only with governmental venality, political anarchy, foreign economic domination, and general national weakness.[11] Coming to the surface during the early 1930s, such a mixture of nationalism, antiliberalism, and idealization of authoritarianism made it perhaps inevitable that Paraguay's nationalist revolution would be influenced in some measure by the broad spectrum of contemporaneous European fascist and corporatist experiments.

At the end of the war, the incumbent Liberal regime of President Eusebio Ayala proved incapable of controlling the wave of popular discontent that swept across Paraguay as the demobilized Chaco forces began to return home. Ayala, a former regional director and vice-president of the International Products Corporation, a New York–based cattle and timber company in Paraguay, had continued to maintain what the United States legation in Asunción described as "close business relations" with the company after becoming Paraguay's chief of state. ("In my conversations with the President," the United States minister to Paraguay reported, "I have little of the feeling of talking to a foreigner. He might be an American lawyer or business man.")[12] In October 1935, Ayala warned his Liberal-dominated Congress that "a deep revolution is taking place within our nation, and day by day it is setting its roots within the popular conscience. We who pretend to inspire these people and guide their destiny must not lock ourselves in outmoded concepts. . . . The country is in a situation that brooks no delay. We must do something and do it soon."[13] The Congress, however, failed to heed Ayala's warning. Instead, it voted down pensions for disabled war veterans, while granting the Liberal commander in chief of the armed forces, General José Félix Estigarribia, an annual pension of 1,500 gold pesos for life and awarding promotions and medals to the sons of prominent Liberal politicians who had seen little front-line action during the war.[14]

In February 1936 the *revolucionarios* struck. Led by young officers from the Chaco, they forcefully seized the government, imprisoned Ayala and Estigarribia,[15] and named Rafael Franco, a popular 39-year-old war hero, as provisional president. Invoking the heritage of Francia and the Lópezes, a "Proclamation of the Liberating Army" announced that the "military arm of the people" had "cast from power . . . the compromised agent of foreign bosses" and his "regime of frock-coated bandits" in order to restore Paraguay "to the level of its past history in the Río de la Plata, to the free dominion over its soil, and to the grandeur of its future."[16]

No sooner had the revolution succeeded, however, than it began to disintegrate. Each of the heterogeneous ideological and factional elements that had joined the *revolucionario* coalition immediately began maneuvering to control the direction and tone of the nationalist revolution to its own advantage. Within Franco's cabinet—itself an unlikely congeries of young authoritarian nationalist military officers, intellectual reformers from Stefanich's Liga Nacional Independiente, "radical" young Colorado and Liberal apostates, and one avowed Marxist—a chaotic power struggle quickly developed for supremacy within the regime. Despite bitterly divisive infighting within the new government, however, Franco's program for the revolution adopted a consistently corporatist orientation. Early measures, in fact, had a decidedly fascist flavor. A March 1936 decree announced that "the liberating revolution in Paraguay is of the same type as the totalitarian social transformations of contemporary Europe, in the sense that the liberating revolution and the State are identical." Declaring that liberalism had been a failure in Paraguay, the regime suspended the constitution of 1870, banned political activity by the traditional parties, outlawed the Communists, and placed all business associations, labor organizations, and "vested interests" under the coordinating supervision of the Ministry of Interior. After mid 1936, as the Stefanich group attained a predominant influence in the cabinet, the government moved steadily toward the creation of a social-welfare state with pronounced corporatist overtones. Government officials spoke increasingly of a "functional, solidary democracy" based on the interests of the workers and peasants. A mild land-redistribution program was launched. Paraguay's first progressive labor legislation was enacted, and the regime encouraged the growth of unions within the structure of a national labor confederation controlled by a newly created Department of Labor. Simultaneously, preparations were begun for a monolithic "national revolutionary party" designed to weld war veterans, students, workers, and peasants together into a power base for a new one-party state.[17]

Within a year, the revolutionary coalition was a shambles. The steady ascension of the Stefanich group within the cabinet estranged most other civilian *revolucionarios* from Franco. Labor leaders appreciated the unprecedented benefits and attention that the regime lavished upon them but stubbornly resisted all efforts by the Department of Labor to subordinate their unions to governmental control, asserting their independence with crippling strikes that kept the economy in constant upheaval. The rural peasantry, long subordinated to the will of local Colorado or Liberal chieftains, remained largely inert and unpoliticized. In addition, the regime's internal schisms, the disruptive labor strikes, and the government's generally radical tone cost Franco the support and respect of many of his fellow *revolucionarios* in the armed-forces officer corps, while an unpopular territorial compromise by Franco's negotiators in the final 1937 Chaco War peace settlement with Bolivia further alienated army sentiment.[18]

With its support thus eroded, the Franco government fell victim to a sudden Liberal counterrevolution. In August 1937, army units led by high-ranking Liberal officers ousted Franco and appointed Félix Paiva, a venerable Liberal, as provisional president. Paiva's first official act was to restore the constitution of 1870.[19]

The Liberals soon learned that a complete restoration of the pre–Chaco War old order was impossible. Labor strikes and student demonstrations kept the nation in a state of continuous upheaval, while from exile Franco's followers organized themselves into the Febrerista party and struck back in a series of unsuccessful countercoups against the new regime.[20] In Asunción, a rival faction of *revolucionario* intellectuals— a small group of devoutly Catholic, Jesuit-trained professors from the business and law faculties of the national university, calling themselves the Tiempistas—issued strident attacks against liberalism and the Liberals from their newspaper *El Tiempo,* advocating a form of Catholic socialism for Paraguay, modeled on Salazar's *Estado novo* in Portugal. Within the armed forces, *revolucionario* officers waited impatiently for an auspicious opportunity to rekindle the nationalist revolution, and the creation in 1938 of the Frente de guerra, a secret lodge of militant, authoritarian nationalist officers, only intensified pervasive rumors of an impending military coup.[21] In July 1938, Paraguay's nervous commercial and industrial interests voluntarily donated $4,000 to Asunción's police chief for the purchase of additional security equipment.[22]

In 1939 elections, the Liberals replaced Paiva with General Estigarribia, in the hope that the former armed-forces commander in chief and Chaco War hero would be able to restore domestic tranquility and discipline in the armed forces. Running unopposed, Estigarribia assumed the presidency in August 1939. For six months he attempted to keep the lid on by means of established constitutional procedures, but a rising crescendo of strikes, demonstrations, and revolutionary plots soon convinced the president and his coterie of young Liberal advisers that drastic measures were required if the Liberals were to maintain themselves in power. In mid February 1940, four days after a nearly successful coup attempt by army elements in league with the Tiempistas, Estigarribia abolished the constitution of 1870, suspended all political activity, and assumed dictatorial powers. Dropping all pretenses of democracy, the Liberal-controlled Congress cleared the way for an overt Liberal dictatorship by voluntarily dissolving itself. Such steps, Estigarribia told the nation, were needed "to conquer the anarchy which threatened to dissolve social ties," and to "perfect democracy."[23] Meanwhile, political dissidents were arrested, and a tight censorship was imposed. Six months later, a new constitution was promulgated. Drawing from Paraguay's authoritarian heritage and from twentieth-century fascist theory,[24] the new constitution of 1940 gave the president virtually limitless powers. The former two-house legislature was replaced by a weak, collaborative Chamber of Deputies and a corporative Council of State composed of the president's cabinet, the archbishop of Paraguay, the president of the central bank, the rector of the national university, and representatives from commerce, agriculture, the processing industries, and the armed forces. Although the new constitution increased the interventionist powers of the state and paid lip service to the social and economic reforms introduced by Franco, the Liberals gave an indication of their essentially conservative, preservationist motives by failing to include a representative from organized labor in the new Council of State. The change in institutions, Estigarribia declared, was more one of organization than of content.[25]

Estigarribia's rise to power coincided with the outbreak of war in Europe, and it was during his presidency that Paraguay was drawn into the rapidly escalating United States–German rivalry for preeminence in southern South America. The German presence in Paraguay on the eve of World War II was substantial. German immigrants had been warmly welcomed in the country since the 1880s, as the Paraguayans struggled to rebuild their population after the near annihilation of the War of the Triple Alliance. By the late 1930s, there were some twenty-six thousand Germans in the country, in a population totaling less than one million. Most had settled in clusters of remote, isolated agricultural colonies in southeastern Paraguay, from Villarrica to beyond Encarnación on the upper Paraná River, where they had built up prosperous small farms and ranches. Those with mechanical skills found a steady demand for their talents in the towns of the region. (Among the early German immigrants in Encarnación was one Hugo Stroessner, who established a brewery, married a Paraguayan woman, and in 1912 fathered a son, Alfredo.)[26] In addition, a German colony numbering some five thousand had established itself in Asunción, and there German businessmen had become an influential element in the local business community, operating a significant percentage of the commercial enterprises in the capital, frequently marrying Paraguayan women, and generally developing influential family and business connections in Asunción society. Although the German communities steadfastly preserved their European cultural identity, retaining German citizenship, continuing to speak their native language, and maintaining their own separate schools, churches, and cultural societies, the Paraguayans tended to hold them in high regard as a group, appreciative of the technical skills, commercial enterprise, and agricultural productivity which they contributed to the national economy.[27]

Hitler's agents enjoyed great success in converting the Paraguayan Germans to National Socialism.[28] It was in Paraguay that the first Latin American branch of the Nazi party was founded, in 1931. By 1937, the German immigrants' extensive system of schools, churches, hospitals, farmers' cooperatives, musical and youth groups, and charitable societies was under the control of Nazi agents working undercover as employees of German firms in Paraguay. Directing all Nazi activities in the country was Reimer Behrens, a cashier at Asunción's German Bank. Among his fellow agents was the pastor of the German Evangelical Church in Asunción, Carlos Richert, who traveled frequently between the capital and German colonies in the interior, carrying messages, showing Nazi propaganda films, and preaching the gospel of National Socialism. The leader of the Hitler Youth in Paraguay, Oskar Ketterer, controlled the entire German school system from his post as principal of Asunción's highly respected Colegio Alemán, which for many years had educated young Asunción Germans and the children of leading Paraguayan families as well. By 1939, Nazi swastikas and portraits of Hitler were being prominently displayed in German schools and business establishments throughout Paraguay. Meanwhile, the German legation in Asunción had launched a relentless propaganda campaign, disseminating pamphlets and newspapers throughout the country, supplying free German news service to local newspapers and free Ufa newsreels to Asunción movie houses, and cultivating young authoritarian nationalist officers in the Paraguayan armed forces at weekly teas and cocktail parties.[29]

In contrast, the United States presence in Paraguay at the start of World War II was negligible. Accounting for less than 1 percent of total United States trade with Latin America and with only three United States business enterprises[30] and fewer than thirty U.S. citizens in the entire country, Paraguay was in fact more remote from United States influence and interest than any other Latin American nation. Nevertheless, during 1938 and 1939, as the Roosevelt administration advanced its program of hemispheric solidarity among the Latin Americans, the increasingly visible German presence in Paraguay began to attract the attention of Washington officials.

From the outset, Estigarribia saw opportunities for both himself and his country to benefit from the escalating international power struggle. While serving, in 1938, as the Paiva government's minister to the United States, he had perceived that United States security apprehensions and desire for Paraguayan support in hemispheric meetings might make the Roosevelt administration receptive to a Paraguayan request for economic aid. In December 1938, he had accordingly handed the Export-Import Bank a request for credits totaling $7.8 million "to improve financial and economic conditions in Paraguay." The key item in Estigarribia's proposal was a $3.3 million credit to construct a 300-mile highway from Asunción east to the Brazilian border at Iguassú. Such a project, Estigarribia told Export-Import Bank president Warren Lee Pierson, would be doubly beneficial: passing through Paraguay's most fertile agricultural region, it would lower farm-to-market freight rates and stimulate production of cotton and other export crops, tripling the volume of Paraguay's exports and reinvigorating her economy. Furthermore, by linking up with the Brazilian highway system, the proposed road would give Paraguay an alternate transportation outlet to the Atlantic, thus breaking the Argentine stranglehold on Paraguay's foreign commerce. In addition, Estigarribia requested $2 million in cash reserves for the Paraguayan Bank of the Republic to shore up Paraguay's unstable currency (only 10 percent of which was backed by gold), $2.5 million for the construction of Asunción's first water and sewage system, and U.S. technical advisers to assist Paraguay in modernizing its agriculture, financial structure, and public-health program.

Estigarribia had more on his mind than Paraguayan economic development, however. By personally negotiating a prestigious foreign-aid package, he hoped to enhance his chances of becoming the Liberal party's candidate for the presidency to succeed Paiva. The requested credits would provide the resources with which, as president, he hoped to stabilize Paraguay's restless political climate. The highway project, he frankly told United States officials, would give employment to a vast number of *revolucionario* war veterans (whom he described as "potential political dynamite"), while the currency-stabilization credit would obviate the need for a devaluation of the Paraguayan peso, thereby avoiding an unpopular and "painful readjustment" of prices and salaries that would inevitably give rise to further political instability.[31]

Estigarribia's assessment of the likelihood of U.S. cooperation was well founded. United States diplomats in Paraguay had viewed the 1936 Franco revolution as an ouster of "the sober thinking and more substantial elements in the country" by "largely untried men, many of . . . distinctly radical tendencies," and the State Department had welcomed the Liberals' return to power in 1937 as "a stabilizing political development."[32] Both Roosevelt and his principal adviser on Latin American affairs, Undersecretary of State Sumner Welles, were particularly impressed with Estigarribia personally as "an intelligent and constructive-minded man" who was "very sincerely desirous of cultivating closer political and economic relations with the United States." Thus, when Estigarribia presented his request for aid, the State Department actively urged the Export-Import Bank to respond favorably, ignoring the conclusion of its own adviser on international economic affairs that "from an economic point of view" the Paraguayan proposal was "at best of dubious advisability" and instead citing "various evidences of European activity in Paraguay at this time," "the caliber of the officials who will be in charge of the development program," and the administration's desire to help Estigarribia "get the [Paraguayan] people's minds off something else" as reasons for granting assistance.[33] As a result, preliminary negotiations toward an aid agreement proceeded without obstacle. By March 1939, Estigarribia was aggressively playing upon his popularity in Washington to strengthen his campaign for the Liberal party's presidential nomination, warning Liberal leaders that U.S. credits would be forthcoming only if he were assured of being Paraguay's next president. Meanwhile, United States officials were watching intently to see "whether the General is strong enough to . . . come through unscathed as the saviour of Paraguay—with American assistance."[34]

In May 1939, however, negotiations were suddenly interrupted by a report that Paraguay was simultaneously engaged in the negotiation of a massive tripartite economic agreement with Germany and Bolivia. The Bolivian government had recently expropriated the Standard Oil Company's holdings in eastern Bolivia without compensation, and Germany was moving quickly to exploit the situation to its own advantage by attempting to gain a monopoly over Bolivian petroleum exports. In an elaborate barter arrangement, the Germans were offering technical and financial assistance to Bolivia's state petroleum agency in the operation of the nationalized oil fields in exchange for Bolivian oil. German assistance was to include the construction of a pipeline from Bolivia eastward to a Paraguayan port on the Paraguay River, whence the oil could be shipped out to Germany. For their part, the Paraguayans were to grant Bolivian oil a preferential position in their domestic markets and assist in its transshipment to Germany. In return, the Germans were offering to build oil refineries in Paraguay and to construct the eastward highway that would link Asunción with Brazil and the Atlantic.[35]

On 24 May 1939, Sumner Welles informed Estigarribia that the United States found the reported project "objectionable in several respects" and indicated his surprise that Paraguay would assist Bolivia in the exploitation of oil fields which the United States still considered to be the legal property of Standard Oil. Countries with undeveloped resources, Welles stated, could hardly expect to attract the capital necessary to develop them unless they gave security to that capital. Estigarribia, who had by now secured the Liberal party's presidential nomination and been elected *in absentia,* assured Welles that, as president, he did not intend to honor the agreement and that "as a matter of policy it was entirely against his own intentions to permit the Government of Paraguay to connive with Bolivia in an endeavor which would be prejudicial to the advancement of liberal trade policies between the American republics and other nations of the world, and in an action taken by the Bolivian Government which had resulted in the confiscation without compensation of American-owned property." "The Minister," Welles recorded, "said that I could be sure that throughout his term of office as President of the Republic the first and foremost principle in his foreign policy would be the development and strengthening of the commercial and political relations between our two countries."[36]

Thus reassured, the Roosevelt administration approved Estigarribia's aid request six days later. The United States agreed to provide $3 million in Export-Import Bank credits for the first phase of the highway project and a $500,000 credit to Paraguay's Bank of the Republic. In addition, technical advisers from the United States Tariff Commission and the Public Health Service were detached to the Paraguayan government. In return, the Paraguayans agreed to award the highway contract to a U.S. engineering firm, to accept an Export-Import Bank representative as a watchdog over the operations of the Bank of the Republic, and generally "to accord every appropriate protection and security to encourage the investment of capital and technical experience of United States citizens in the development of Paraguay's natural resources."[37] As a triumphant Estigarribia prepared to return to Paraguay to begin his presidency, the Roosevelt administration and the New York banking community each feted their new-found client at sumptuous honorary banquets.[38]

The early months of Estigarribia's presidency were times of relative prosperity for Paraguay. Initially, the war in Europe produced a record demand by the belligerents for Paraguayan meat products, timber, and leather-tanning exports. By mid 1940, however, the German occupation of western Europe and naval warfare in the Atlantic had sharply restricted Paraguay's European export markets, seriously undercutting Estigarribia's government—which depended upon customs duties for 70 percent of its fiscal revenues. During the first half of 1940, Paraguayan exports declined by 30 percent, and as the domestic economy reeled from the impact of a devastating trade deficit, Estigarribia began to intensify his commitment to hemispheric solidarity in the expectation of securing further economic favors from the United States.[39]

The Paraguayan delegation to the August 1940 Havana Conference

Signing of United States–Paraguayan economic-aid agreement, Department of State, Washington, D.C., 13 June 1939. Seated (*left to right*): Paraguayan Minister to the United States José Félix Estigarribia; Secretary of State Cordell Hull. Standing (*left to right*): Herbert Feis, State Department economic adviser; Emilio Collado, officer—State Department's Division of American Republics; Jesse Jones, chairman of the Reconstruction Finance Corporation; Laurence Duggan, chief of the State Department's Division of American Republics; Henry Morgenthau, Jr., secretary of the treasury; Warren Lee Pierson, president of the Export-Import Bank; Sumner Welles, undersecretary of state; Pablo Max Insfran, counselor of the Paraguayan Legation. (Courtesy of United Press International.)

was sent with instructions "to cooperate in the closest possible manner" with United States representatives. Visiting Washington after the conference, Estigarribia's foreign minister told Sumner Welles that Paraguay desired "to cooperate to the fullest extent with the United States on all matters, whether they related to political or economic questions or to the question of military defense of the Western Hemisphere," but that Paraguay was also "looking to the United States for assistance in its . . . economic distress." The assistance already tendered, the foreign minister continued, "had been of the utmost value but . . . the economic situation on account of the World War was constantly deteriorating," and Paraguay "hoped the . . . United States would be able to extend further cooperation." On 20 August 1940, Estigarribia informed the United States minister in Paraguay that a German "fifth column" was fomenting "intrigues in the Army" and that he intended to personally "admonish" the German minister regarding Nazi activities in Paraguay. The president quickly added that he was also "greatly preoccupied" with "finances," and that he desired the United States' "opinion" of a soon-to-be-completed "plan to relieve the situation." Ten days later, Paraguay presented the United States with a request for $17 million in economic assistance. Among the component items were $2 million in stabilization credits for the Bank of the Republic, $3 million to enable the government to purchase Paraguay's rapidly accumulating surplus of export products, $5 million for additional highway construction, and $2.6 million for "sanitary works" in Asunción. In return, Estigarribia offered to grant United States military forces air-base rights on Paraguayan territory in the event that hemispheric defense operations became necessary. "It would seem," the United States legation in Asunción informed the State Department, "that the matter of hemisphere defense and financial stability of the Paraguayan Government [may] be considered as more or less related."[40]

By early September, the German minister to Paraguay was expressing displeasure at Estigarribia's close friendship with the United States, warning that "upon termination of the war Germany would not forget how Paraguay had acted." Remarking that he did not "relish threats," Estigarribia told the United States minister that "as soon as a definite understanding" on United States economic assistance had been reached, he intended to "do something more than merely admonish the German minister." The president was to have no further opportunities to serve the cause of hemispheric solidarity, however. On 7 September 1940, three weeks after promulgating the constitution which institutionalized a Liberal-party dictatorship in Paraguay and two weeks after determining to curb German activities in the country, Estigarribia was killed in an airplane crash while flying to a weekend resort east of Asunción. Although no evidence of assassination came to light, the British Foreign Office speculated that "perhaps the death of the President was not due to pure accident," while in Washington the State Department received vague rumors that an autopsy had revealed traces of poison in the body of the plane's pilot.[41]

Revolucionario elements in the armed forces now moved swiftly to take advantage of Estigarribia's death. Confronting the fallen president's cabinet in the national palace at midnight of September seventh, authoritarian nationalist army officers demanded that one of their colleagues, General Higinio Morínigo, be named provisional president to fill out Estigarribia's term. The stunned Liberals, unwilling to risk a power showdown with the army and perhaps believing that they could manipulate Morínigo, acceded.[42] A new phase of the Paraguayan nationalist revolution had begun—and with it, the orientation of Paraguay's foreign policy was to change significantly.

5

Bad Neighbor in Paraguay:
Higinio Morínigo
and World War II

Higinio Morínigo dominated Paraguayan politics from 1940 to 1948, remaining in power longer than any other Paraguayan chief of state between Francisco Solano López and Alfredo Stroessner. Born near Paraguarí in 1897, the man who was to lead Paraguay through the turbulent years of World War II and the early Cold War had close personal links with Paraguay's pre-1870 authoritarian heritage. One of his grandfathers had been killed and the other wounded in the War of the Triple Alliance, and his father had been wounded and taken prisoner as a boy of eleven serving in the Paraguayan army during the desperate last phases of the fighting. A merchant by profession, the father had moved the family to Asunción in 1906, and there Morínigo entered the national military academy. His subsequent career exemplified the evolution of a middle-class army officer into a leading authoritarian nationalist political figure by the late 1930s.[1]

As a young junior officer, Morínigo had been ordered to participate in a violent civil insurrection in 1922 involving rival factions of the ruling Liberal party, an experience which embittered him toward civilian politicians and their habitual practice of embroiling the army in their domestic power struggles. Subsequent assignments to remote frontier forts revealed to him the national government's neglect of border defenses and exposed him to the appallingly primitive living conditions that Paraguayan troops were forced to endure. A brief assignment as a regional field commander during the Chaco War gave him his opportunity for rapid advancement. In 1936, the Franco regime promoted Morínigo to colonel and appointed him as commander of the important northern garrison at Concepción, in which capacity he headed a highly publicized 1936 expedition to Cerro Corá that retrieved the remains of Francisco Solano López and returned them to the National Pantheon of Heroes in Asunción. After Franco's overthrow, Morínigo's popularity among the growing *revolucionario* faction of the officer corps continued to rise, and from that power base he gained the post of army chief of staff in 1938. In an address to the officers of the Army-Navy Center in November of that year, Morínigo outlined his political views and those of the nationalistic younger officers for whom he was increasingly becoming a spokesman. The "sterile quarrels" of Paraguay's "public men," he charged, were destroying the nation's population and wealth. The continual coups and revolutions had given rise to an "alarming exodus of our countrymen to neighboring countries," while the "indifference" of Paraguay's "men of government" had permitted "the foreigner" to occupy a "privileged position" in the national economy. The civilian politicians, he continued, were also destroying the professional integrity of the Paraguayan military:

> The armed forces are inseparably associated with the very life of the nation, and . . . to convert them into an instrument of the political party constitutes a crime against the country; it is the same as conspiring against the nation. . . .
>
> The chaotic state of domestic politics . . . has permeated the army, dividing the officer corps into contesting bands fighting against each other. The results are obvious: ruin and discredit for the nation; prison and loss of career for the defeated. And all for what? The condition of the country does not improve. After every change of government the status quo persists. What value is it for us to divide into factions to help men or political groups come to power in direct prejudice to the unity of the officer corps and the destruction and disorganization of our army? We must put an end to this state of things. . . . I tell you, my compatriots, we must unify ourselves once and for all and march as one man toward the conquest of the days of grandeur, of prosperity, and of happiness for our heroic Paraguayan nation.[2]

Calling for a larger, more modern, and professionalized army, Morínigo quoted the Argentine authoritarian ideologue Gustavo Martínez Zuviría to the effect that "the rights of a people not supported by the sword are nothing more than aspirations about which the poets sing."[3]

As a conciliatory gesture to the restless *revolucionario* elements in the army, Paiva took Morínigo into his cabinet as minister of the interior for a brief period in early 1939, and Morínigo lost no time in emphasizing, in a nationwide radio address to the Paraguayan people, that he represented no political party or group but belonged only to "the incorruptible, glorious National Army, defender of the nation and of public order." "The armed forces of the nation," he warned, "[are] today more than ever united and determined to give the country a National Government without party banners. . . . The painful experiences of civil wars and *cuartelazos* [are] repudiated in the minds of this generation of officers and leaders. The hour has arrived in which, if political parties wish to exist, they must . . . give up forever the practice of manipulating the barracks to assist their rise to power."[4] In May 1940, army pressure forced Estigarribia to accept Morínigo as his minister of war, and it was from that position that Morínigo was forced upon the Liberals as Estigarribia's successor in September 1940.

As president, Morínigo immediately established a regime based on the support of authoritarian nationalist elements in the armed forces. Leading *revolucionario* officers were brought into the cabinet, and militantly nationalistic young officers—most of whom were captains and majors affiliated with the secret Frente de guerra lodge—were rapidly promoted and placed in key military and police commands. Three of Morínigo's most loyal personal supporters from the Frente de guerra— Majors Bernardo Aranda, Pablo Stagni, and Victoriano Benítez Vera— were elevated to the rank of lieutenant colonel and given influential assignments as army chief of staff, commander of the air force, and First Cavalry division commander, respectively. By tradition, the cavalry command was particularly crucial to any regime's survival in power. Stationed on the outskirts of Asunción at Campo Grande, Paraguay's principal military and air base, the cavalry guarded the capital and controlled the national military arsenals. With his protégé Benítez Vera as its commander, Morínigo frankly labeled it his "praetorian guard."[5]

At the same time, however, Morínigo conceded the need for trained civilian assistance to staff and run the complex machinery of government. Initially, he turned for civilian administrative guidance to both the Febreristas and the Tiempistas, who had joined together in a short-lived coalition of civilian *revolucionario* forces. On entering the government, however, the Febreristas devoted most of their energies to plotting the removal of Morínigo and the restoration of Rafael Franco to power, and after weathering an April 1941 Febrerista coup attempt (during which he was forced to seek temporary refuge in the cavalry division's barracks at Campo Grande), Morínigo relied solely upon the Tiempistas as his civilian advisers. A small group of able, conscientious Catholic activists from the national university, closely allied with the Paraguayan Church hierarchy, the Tiempistas thereafter controlled the key civilian portfolios in Morínigo's cabinet—with the movement's leaders, Carlos Andrada and Luis Argaña, receiving the ministries of interior and foreign relations respectively.[6]

In welding together an armed-forces–Tiempista coalition for his power base, Morínigo had assembled a regime of earnest and idealistic authoritarians. Politically, both groups tended to equate democracy with the corrupt and chaotic "democratic" party governments of Paraguay's post-1870 era. As an alternative, Morínigo's military supporters openly advocated a permanent military dictatorship, directed by honest, patriotic military officers and inspired by the developmental authoritarianism of Paraguay's pre-1870 "golden age." In a March 1941 public oath of loyalty to Morínigo and the Paraguayan nationalist revolution (which they defined as "inspired by the austere patriotism and authentic nationalism of the great governors who forged the strong and worthy Paraguay of the past, Rodríguez de Francia, Carlos Antonio López, and Francisco Solano López"), the Asunción officer corps charged that "the liberal system of government has been the principal cause of the political anarchy, of the economic misery, and the material backwardness of the Nation" and asserted their conviction that "the professional politicians who incarnated that unfortunate regime must be reduced to impotency." The Tiempistas, for their part, were zealous advocates of "good government" and favored a paternalistic "social Catholic" dictatorship for Paraguay modeled on the "new states" of Salazar in Portugal and Vargas in Brazil. Upon becoming Morínigo's minister of the interior, Andrada, the Tiempistas' leading theoretician, immediately departed on a three-month visit to Brazil to study the governmental methods and institutional structures of Vargas's *Estado novo,* while in Asunción, the Tiempista newspaper issued daily editorial attacks against liberalism as a system which was "in complete bankruptcy throughout the world, has always been divorced from national reality, and is absolutely incapable of satisfying its most legitimate aspirations."[7]

Shortly after taking office, Morínigo issued a series of public pronouncements that defined the nationalist revolution and indicated the ideological orientation that it could be expected to take under his leadership. "The Paraguayan Nationalist Revolution," he said, "came into being as a virile . . . protest against the old, worn-out procedures of the professional political oligarchy, which knew only how to ruin and bleed the Republic in cruel fratricidal wars undertaken to conduct absurd conflicts of personal power." Dedicating his government to "the arduous and magnificent labor of National Reconstruction," Morínigo promised a program of authoritarian modernization and reform for Paraguay:

> As regards the State's functions . . . we believe that the true and
> direct object of the State is the development of all the faculties of the
> nation and the perfecting of its life. Hence we reject Liberalism, the
> product of the 19th century, which does not admit the intervention of

the State positively in satisfying human needs and considerably reduces its mission. We stand for intervention above all in the economic field, especially in the relations between capital and labor to correct social injustice. The inertia of the Liberal State must give way to the dynamism of the protecting and directing State.[8]

The new order in Paraguay was to be openly and unapologetically authoritarian. Reconstruction would be accomplished through a "forced march of the country," Morínigo announced; "as descendants of the lineage of the Lópezes, all Paraguayans . . . must dispose themselves to accept without murmurings or protests the decisions of the government." Declaring that "an exclusively electoral democracy in a country not educated for a conscientious and free vote is a farce," Morínigo pledged to instill in the Paraguayan people "a new civic mentality based on the ideas of duty and responsibility." "The ranking place of national interest over the selfish and sordid interest of individuals," he said, "constitutes a fundamental political principle of the Paraguayan Nationalist Revolution." The "countersign of the Revolution," he announced, would be "DISCIPLINE, HIERARCHY, ORDER."[9]

The authoritarian nature of the new regime quickly revealed itself to Paraguay's traditional political parties. In December 1940 the top leaders of the Liberal party were summarily arrested and relegated to remote "detention camps" in northern Paraguay. Shortly thereafter, a government decree-law declared the party illegal. When the Colorado party publicly protested the government's restrictions in mid 1941, the leading Colorado officials were also imprisoned.[10]

The essence of the regime's social philosophy was also revealed in December 1940, when Morínigo publicly pledged to "raise the worker's standard of living, encourage his integral improvement, and impede the entrance of alien elements and agitators of the professional type in the workmen's syndicates." Subsequently, Morínigo launched a series of social programs beneficial to Paraguay's working classes, establishing Paraguay's first social-security program and a minimum-wage law, constructing some fifty-two schools and twenty-nine regional hospitals, and ordering the country's processing industries to provide health clinics for their workers. At the same time, however, the regime was moving to increase its control over organized labor, and when Paraguay's labor unions called a nationwide general strike against government intervention in January 1941, Morínigo broke it with a ruthless application of military force, imprisoned its leaders, dissolved the national labor confederation, and imposed a tight supervisory control over the election of union officials.[11]

The new regime's most radical initiatives, however, came in the field of economic policy. As president, Morínigo spoke frequently of his determination to restore the state-controlled economy of the pre-1870 era, and his initial public addresses were filled with nationalistic attacks on foreign capital. Foreign "enterprises exploiting concessions or public services," he warned, could anticipate "permanent State intervention and control."[12] In December 1940, during his third month in office, Morínigo gave dramatic substance to such rhetoric by suddenly nationalizing the United States–owned Asunción Port Concession Corporation and placing the capital's vital port facility under the control of the new state-owned Asunción Port Administration. Only after lengthy and bitter negotiations with corporation officials and State Department representatives did he agree to provide partial compensation. Two months later, in February 1941, a comprehensive new exchange-control law placed all of Paraguay's international trade and foreign-exchange transactions under the control of the Bank of the Republic, in effect establishing a state trading monopoly. The exchange-control law also "nationalized" Paraguay's monetary system. So unstable had the Paraguayan peso become that few citizens were willing to accept it as currency, and Argentine pesos instead circulated freely throughout the country as an accepted medium of exchange. By prohibiting commercial transactions in any but Paraguayan currency, the new law terminated this infringement of national sovereignty, and eventually Morínigo was able to stabilize Paraguay's monetary system and replace the peso with a sound new national unit of currency: the guaraní. The exchange-control law was soon followed by other state-imposed economic innovations, including mandatory domestic price ceilings on all commodities and an unprecedented corporate income tax on all foreign and domestic business enterprises in Paraguay.[13] As a result, the United States legation reported, "a great many persons here, especially those possessing property or engaged in business . . . are very apprehensive of the future." "Most upper-class Paraguayans," it added, "are antagonistic to the present government."[14]

As the nationalization of the United States–owned port facility indicated, Morínigo's foreign-policy orientation differed considerably from that of his predecessor, Estigarribia. Neither the Paraguayan armed forces nor the Tiempistas had any particular affinity for the cause of the democracies at the start of World War II. Most Paraguayan military officers were in fact fervent admirers of the German armed forces, and Morínigo later admitted that his close circle of Frente de guerra military supporters was "sympathetic to Germany during the war."[15] The course of the war during 1939, 1940, and 1941 had persuaded a majority of the officer corps that a German military victory might well be inevitable, a prediction constantly reiterated by Germany's effective propaganda campaign, which had also converted many Paraguayan officers to the belief that, based on the historical record, the true "imperialists" in the Western Hemisphere were Great Britain and the United States rather than Germany. Such views were reinforced among Paraguayan officers by the presence of a Vichy French military mission—the only foreign military mission in Paraguay at the start of World War II. Popular and influential, the Vichy advisers openly endorsed a policy of collaboration with Germany from their posts as training instructors at the national military academy.[16] At the same time, Morínigo's Tiempista supporters freely admitted that there were "a number of points of contact" between their ideology and the totalitarian doctrines of Germany and Italy. The new minister of foreign relations, Tiempista leader Luis Argaña, stated frankly that he did not consider the Axis powers to be a serious threat to the Western Hemisphere and that "even if England fell," Germany would be "too preoccupied" with rebellions and hostilities in occupied Europe "to threaten the Americas either economically or militarily." Furthermore, Argaña and the Tiempistas shared with their military colleagues in the regime a conviction that, in the event of a total Axis victory, an authoritarian military-Tiempista dictatorship in Paraguay would "be left quite independent because of the sympathetic bond created by kindred ideals" and that in the end, Paraguay might even "fare very well in a totalitarian world."[17]

To a large extent, the lower echelons of the new government were dominated by pro-Axis nationalists. The chief of the national police force, Colonel Mutshuito Villasboa, a founder of the Frente de guerra, was an ardent Axis sympathizer who had named his son Adolfo Hirohito in homage to two of the most renowned Axis personages. The director of the national police academy, Captain Rolando degli Uberti, was an Italian-Paraguayan active in Mussolini's Fascist party; under Uberti's direction, Paraguayan police cadets were soon displaying Nazi swastikas and Italian flag insignia on their uniforms. The head of Morínigo's secret police, Marcos Fuster, was an intimate friend of the leading Nazi agents in Paraguay and, together with Uberti, belonged to a mysterious Nazi underground action-group, the Ring of Sacrifice. Morínigo's official secretary, Ricardo Brugada Doldán, and the head of the army's secret police, Captain Plutarco Mello Vargas, both openly admitted pro-Axis sympathies, while Foreign Minister Argaña's chief assistant, Undersecretary of Foreign Relations Armín Seifart Centurión, was the son of a German immigrant, had studied for eight years in Germany, and was an attorney for several large German firms in Paraguay.[18]

Under the guiding influence of the new regime, Paraguayan public opinion on international matters soon shifted sharply toward a pro-Axis point of view. The Liberal party newspaper, *El País*—Paraguay's leading daily and an outspoken champion of United States–Paraguayan cooperation throughout Estigarribia's presidency—was confiscated by the government in January 1941 and placed under the editorial control of a former staff member of the German legation in Asunción. Thereafter, *El País* slanted its headlines and foreign news coverage in an overtly pro-German manner and took every opportunity to deride "decadent, capitalist democracy" in favor of the "authoritative state." Of Asunción's other two daily newspapers, *La Tribuna* was directly subsidized by the German legation and openly espoused the Axis cause, while the official government organ, *La Razón* (formerly the Tiempistas' *El Tiempo*), disparaged "electoral democracy" and spoke favorably of the advantages of commercial cooperation with Germany. Meanwhile, the German propaganda campaign intensified noticeably. "Paraguay has offered a free field to German pamphlet and news propaganda," the United States legation informed Washington in mid 1941, "and the Germans are laboring in it tirelessly, intelligently, and successfully" to the point where they "are taking over the public mind." "The atmosphere here," the United States minister reported with alarm in August 1941, "is far less favorable to the democracies than was the case a year ago, and the government officials, army officers, and younger businessmen are coming to feel that Germany's victory is inevitable and will have beneficial results for South America and for Paraguay." "It would look," the legation remarked, "as if the influence of the United States had now reached a new low."[19]

In Washington, U.S. officials watched with growing concern as Paraguay slipped rapidly out of the United States orbit. In determining an effective response to the radically changing atmosphere in Asunción, the Roosevelt administration pondered the question of "whether it is more expedient to await a change . . . of regime and some sure evidence of willingness and ability to go along with the United States in the program of continental solidarity . . . or to go on granting credits . . . in the hope that the reaction to such largesse will be what is desired and that Paraguay will become a sure friend of the United States in South America."[20] By early 1941, the administration had concluded that the latter alternative was the most promising course of action. The United States would attempt to lure Paraguay back into its orbit by cultivating the Morínigo regime with offers of foreign aid.

In improving relations with Morínigo, however, the first prerequisite for the Roosevelt administration was a change in United States diplomatic personnel in Paraguay. During his five years in the country, United States minister Findley Howard had formed extremely close ties with the leaders of the traditional Paraguayan political parties, and his inability to conceal his disdain for the *revolucionario* factions who now controlled the government had severely strained his relations with the new regime. In addition, Howard's notorious alcoholic excesses and occasional public nudity were the cause of widespread scandal in Asunción society, further alienating the new government, whose Tiempista and military leaders were considered "almost ascetically abstemious in their personal habits." As a result, Howard had almost immediately

Findley Howard. (Courtesy of United Press International.)

67

become *persona non grata* with Morínigo, and the State Department quickly replaced him early in 1941.[21]

The next U.S. move to cultivate Morínigo took the form of a humanitarian gesture. Learning that Morínigo's ten-year-old son suffered from infantile paralysis, Sumner Welles suggested to Roosevelt in February 1941 that the United States offer to provide the boy with medical treatment. "Since the death of . . . Estigarribia," Welles said, "the internal situation in Paraguay has been steadily deteriorating. . . . If the boy . . . came in this way to the United States, the President would have a far better reason to think well of us, and he would be consequently less likely to fall under the Axis influence." "I am sure," Welles added, "that an expenditure of this kind could legitimately be regarded as coming within the purview of . . . defense funds." The idea struck Roosevelt as "excellent," and U.S. officials were soon dispatched to escort Morínigo's wife and son to Roosevelt's Warm Springs, Georgia, hydro-therapeutic center, where the boy received three months of highly successful therapy.[22]

Simultaneously, the administration dangled offers of economic assistance in front of Morínigo. Throughout 1941, the Export-Import Bank repeatedly declared its willingness to provide Paraguay with some $900,000 in new credits for highway construction, agricultural development, or port improvements, while the State Department hinted at the possibility of a $4 million credit for an Asunción water-and-sewage system. Morínigo, however, responded to these enticements "with no very outstanding show of warmth." Visiting Asunción in April 1941, Export-Import Bank president Pierson had a "stormy interview" with Paraguayan officials, in which "both sides said sharp things." The Paraguayans expressed interest only in the possibility of obtaining United States financing for a complex of refrigerated storage warehouses to protect Paraguayan export-crop surpluses from spoilage, and enthusiastically showed Pierson detailed construction blueprints calling for German cold-storage equipment and the services of a German contractor from Buenos Aires. Frustrated, State Department officials were soon complaining of Morínigo's "lack of appreciation" for United States aid offers, expressing irritation at his failure to perceive that "hearty collaboration in the cause of hemisphere solidarity" would be rewarded with United States assistance "in every practicable manner."[23]

A different type of inducement, however, swiftly produced an initial breakthrough for the United States. "The thing . . . which would be right up this government's alley would be something military," legation officials had hypothesized in April 1941, and accordingly, the Roosevelt administration had quickly extended to Morínigo an offer of some $11 million worth of lend-lease military equipment, under terms described by the State Department as "by far the most generous of our lend-lease offers to the other American Republics." Morínigo accepted at once, unable to resist such an auspicious opportunity to refurbish his armed forces and strengthen the Campo Grande army units on which his power base rested. The State Department immediately moved to exploit this first opening wedge by suggesting to Morínigo that the Paraguayan armed forces would not derive "maximum advantage" from the United States equipment unless he would "agree to replace the French Military Mission with a group of American instructors."[24]

The unexpected Japanese attack on Pearl Harbor in December 1941 abruptly forced the Morínigo regime and other publicly uncommitted South American governments to make hard and unequivocating foreign-policy commitments for the first time since the outbreak of hostilities. As an active belligerent in the war, the United States immediately summoned the Latin Americans to an emergency consultative meeting of hemispheric foreign ministers at Rio de Janeiro in January 1942, where each Latin American government was pressed to state its alignment in the international power struggle. Rejecting a British suggestion that the United States join with Great Britain "in working up a series of Latin American coup d'états" against uncooperative regimes,[25] the Roosevelt administration instead chose to ply Latin American delegations at the Rio Conference with offers of economic aid, in return for which the Latin Americans were requested to demonstrate their solidarity with the United States by severing diplomatic relations with the Axis powers and restricting Axis commercial and espionage activities in their countries.[26]

After considerable internal debate, Getúlio Vargas's Brazilian regime ultimately opted for hemispheric solidarity, calculating that the flow of United States economic and military aid which could thus be obtained would tip the Brazilian-Argentine balance of power in South America permanently in Brazil's favor, enabling it to achieve preeminence among the Latin American nations. Vargas's expectations did not go unfulfilled. In exchange for his support at Rio, the Roosevelt administration agreed to provide Brazil with $200 million worth of lend-lease military hardware and some $126 million in development credits.[27]

The Argentine government of Ramón Castillo, in contrast, chose to maintain Argentina's traditional foreign policy of independent neutrality, refusing to be drawn into the United States orbit at Rio despite pointed U.S. warnings to Argentine delegates that United States "economic and financial assistance" would "be given only to those nations which are whole-heartedly and effectively cooperating with us in the defense of the hemisphere." Under intense pressure from authoritarian nationalist military elements at home, the Argentine delegation effectively obstructed any final conference resolution stronger than one merely "recommending" that the American republics break diplomatic relations with the Axis nations.[28] Argentina, Foreign Minister Enrique Ruiz Guiñazú explained shortly after the conference, belonged to the European economic sphere and looked upon the expansion of United States military, economic, and political strength as a greater menace than that of Nazi Germany.[29]

In Asunción, the startling news of Pearl Harbor immediately set in motion a heated foreign-policy debate within Morínigo's government. Leading military officers urged that Paraguay should "wait for some months to ascertain the probable course of events before compromising itself against the Axis powers." The Tiempistas, on the other hand, argued that under existing conditions, Paraguay had "no practical alternative" but to cooperate with the Allies. In a series of emotional mid-December meetings with groups of Paraguayan officers, Foreign Minister Argaña stressed that due to inevitable British and U.S. naval supremacy in the Atlantic, it would be "at least three or four years" before German economic cooperation was "likely to be feasible" and that during this period, the United States would be Paraguay's only available source of military and economic aid.[30] When, in the course of one such meeting, General Juan B. Ayala vehemently pronounced himself "one hundred per cent sympathetic to the Axis cause," Argaña allegedly responded that Ayala had

> expressed the sentiments of all those present. . . . The Axis powers know full well what Paraguay's real sentiments are and will take that into consideration when they finally triumph. But in the meanwhile it is imperative that Paraguay play along with the United States for urgent reasons of national self-interest.[31]

The Tiempistas' views eventually prevailed, and armed with the reluctant acquiescence of the Paraguayan officer corps, Argaña enthusiastically pledged Paraguay's adherence to the cause of hemispheric solidarity at the Rio Conference. Ten weeks later, the Morínigo regime presented Washington officials with a request for $7 million in economic aid.[32] The United States had gained an ally.

6

The United States, Morínigo, and the Economic Development of Paraguay

Morínigo modeled his economic-development program on the self-contained, state-controlled economy of the pre-1870 authoritarian state.[1] There was no need to look to foreign sources for a development plan, he told the nation; the new "revolutionary Government" would simply "return to the customs of nationalism inspired in the work of the great statesman who built our country, making it great, strong, and prosperous . . . Carlos Antonio López." New state monopolies would recover sovereignty over the nation's alienated natural resources. Domestic production of Paraguay's agricultural, pastoral, and forest products would be expanded to make the nation again self-sufficient in essential raw materials and foodstuffs. Industrial-development projects would be undertaken to diversify the economy and put an end to foreign economic domination. Implicit in the regime's economic-development program was a rejection of laissez-faire capitalism in favor of a return to the traditional mixed economy of Paraguay's colonial and early national periods, an economy in which the state assumed a pervasive and permanent interventionist role vis-à-vis the private sector—planning and co-ordinating, regulating, and, where necessary, actually producing. Private property would be respected, Morínigo said, but it would henceforth be subject to the "direction and regulatory action" of the "dynamic State."

As a first priority, the government moved to reinvigorate agriculture. Although Paraguay's fertile soil and warm climate gave the nation a potentially rich agricultural base, domestic production of the country's principal crops—wheat, tobacco, cotton, tea, and fruit—had remained stagnant since the War of the Triple Alliance. Most of the nation's productive land was owned by foreign timber and cattle companies and a small handful of upper-class Paraguayan ranchers, and actual crop-farming was left, for the most part, to peasant sharecroppers and poor rural squatters, who lacked even the most rudimentary agricultural implements and produced at a bare subsistence level. Government studies during the early 1940s found that two-thirds of Paraguay's farmers were without plows of any type, and that only one in a hundred owned a mule. In an effort to stimulate agriculture, Morínigo's state agricultural bank purchased surplus domestic crops at guaranteed high prices, providing a financial incentive for farmers to expand production and modernize their methods of cultivation. Selling the accumulated commodities in foreign markets when world prices reached sufficiently profitable levels, the government then funneled the resulting foreign-exchange earnings into a "supervised credit program" that enabled farmers to purchase modern equipment and supplies from the state on easy credit terms. In its long-range impact, Morínigo's agricultural-assistance program was designed to encourage the eventual emergence of an agrarian middle sector of independent, medium-sized capitalist farmers, although the regime also established a series of experimental peasant cooperatives, relocating several thousand rural squatters into state-owned agricultural colonies on previously unexploited land expropriated from foreign owners.

Morínigo also placed great emphasis on industrial development. Rather than envisioning the creation of industries to manufacture steel or other heavy capital goods in Paraguay, however, his industrialization program was a modest and pragmatic one, realistically attuned to Paraguay's essentially agrarian economic base. For seventy years, the products of Paraguay's forests and fields had flowed out of the country as raw, unprocessed bulk exports, only to return eventually in the form of high-cost finished imports. To remedy this situation, Morínigo proposed to establish small, domestically owned processing industries that could exploit Paraguay's raw materials for national consumption, thereby reducing dependence on costly foreign imports and retaining a larger share of the country's natural wealth within its own borders. Among the projects to be introduced were lumber and paper-products industries for Paraguay's timber resources, dairy and leather-goods industries for its livestock herds, textile and flour mills for its cotton and wheat crops, canning factories for its fruit orchards, a cigarette industry for its tobacco crop, a cement plant, brick factories, and vegetable-oil processing plants.

Wherever possible, the regime sought to induce private Paraguayan capital to undertake the desired industrialization projects, using incentives such as a 1942 "industrial privilege" law, which granted monopoly status and tax exemptions to domestic entrepreneurs who established the first industrial enterprise in a field approved by the government. Where necessary, however, the state was prepared to play the role of entrepreneur in its own right, drawing inspiration from the earlier authoritarian state of the pre-1870 era. Deliberately emulating the early national dictators, Morínigo established new state-owned ranches, state sawmills, and state quarries in Paraguay, placing them under the direction of the armed forces. The first state industrial monopoly appeared in December 1941, with the creation of the National Alcohol Corporation (COPAL). Monopolizing the production, distillation, and sale of industrial alcohol, *caña* (sugar-cane rum), and sugar, COPAL revitalized Paraguay's small alcohol and sugar industries by increasing production and regulating quality. Several months later, the Paraguayan Meat Corporation (COPACAR) was formed. A joint, mixed venture of the state and private Paraguayan cattlemen, COPACAR was designed to compete with, and eventually oust, the British and United States companies that dominated Paraguay's livestock and meat-packing industries.

Stimulated by government incentives, as well as by Allied purchases of raw materials after Pearl Harbor, Paraguay's economic output rose sharply under Morínigo. The country's export sales increased by some 223 percent between 1939 and 1945 (see table 4), and under the careful management of the Bank of the Republic, acting as a state trading agency, Paraguay's balance of trade moved from deficit to surplus (see table 5). The resulting exchange revenues were used to finance agricultural modernization programs, import-substitution projects, and increased social-service expenditures.

In carrying out the minor "industrial revolution" needed to structurally transform Paraguay's economy, however, Morínigo encountered obstacles of overwhelming magnitude. To sustain new industries, internal and external consumer markets for Paraguayan processed goods were

TABLE 4

PRINCIPAL PARAGUAYAN EXPORTS, 1939 AND 1945

COMMODITY	1939 (In Millions)	1945 (In Millions)
Cattle products	$3.254	$7.066
Timber products	2.706	7.093
Cotton	.973	3.454
Tobacco	.288	1.229

SOURCES: United States, Department of Commerce, *Foreign Commerce Yearbook, 1939* (Washington, D.C.: Government Printing Office, 1942), p. 211; and ibid., *1948* (Washington, D.C.: Government Printing Office, 1950), p. 384.

TABLE 5

PARAGUAYAN BALANCE OF TRADE, 1940 AND 1945

YEAR	EXPORTS (In Millions)	IMPORTS (In Millions)
1940	$ 5.9	$ 7.7
1945	22.3	17.7

SOURCE: United States, Department of Commerce, *Foreign Commerce Yearbook, 1948* (Washington, D.C.: Government Printing Office, 1950), p. 383.

necessary, and the development of such markets was in turn predicated upon a massive restructuring of Paraguay's transportation networks. New roads were needed to link Paraguay's isolated rural masses to regional marketing centers, enabling farmers to sell more crops, generating more rural income, and raising domestic purchasing power to levels capable of supporting native industries. In addition, for new Paraguayan products to be commercially competitive in foreign markets, new avenues of international transportation were needed to free Paraguayan exports from dependence on the slow and prohibitively expensive British-owned railroad and Argentine shipping line which carried the country's products south to Buenos Aires, Paraguay's only existing outlet to world markets. Industrialization also necessitated the development of new domestic sources of energy. The country's power supply in the early 1940s was inadequate to meet even existing requirements, depending exclusively on the limited productive output of a few ancient wood- and charcoal-burning electric generators. Even in the capital, electricity was available to less than a quarter of the populace. Morínigo fervently hoped that Paraguay's western Chaco region would eventually yield vast petroleum deposits which would provide unlimited energy resources to fuel new enterprises, but preliminary geological surveys and exploratory drilling lay well beyond the financial and technological capacity of his regime. Nor did the country possess the skilled labor force needed to manage and operate new industries. Technicians and training instructors would initially have to be brought in from more advanced countries to assist the Paraguayans in establishing even a limited industrial base.

The primary impediment to Paraguayan industrial development, however—and the one upon which all the other obstacles ultimately rested—was a lack of development capital. Despite the government's investment incentives, private Paraguayan capitalists remained reluctant to accept the risks of long-term entrepreneurial investment in new industries, particularly in view of Paraguay's chronic political and fiscal instability, and instead maintained their preference for more traditional investment opportunities, notably real estate and Argentine government bonds. Furthermore, Paraguay's commercial banks were all foreign-owned and were notorious for charging exorbitant mortgage and interest rates on speculative investment loans. In an effort to raise capital, Morínigo imposed a 6 to 10 percent corporate income tax, but Paraguay's domestic tax base was simply too weak and underdeveloped to supply sufficient levels of development funds. Thus, Morínigo quickly came to share with other twentieth-century "third-world" leaders the basic dilemma of underdevelopment: to finance the economic-development programs that would free Paraguay from its dependence on foreign capital, he was forced to turn for financial assistance to the capital-exporting nations that already held a dominant position in the world economy.

In April 1942, shortly after the Rio Conference, the Morínigo regime accordingly presented its $7 million foreign-aid request to United States officials in Washington. Specifically, the Paraguayans requested Export-Import Bank credits of $2.8 million for highway construction, $2.1 million for "industrial plants" and a "petroleum survey," and $2.1 million for "sanitary works." Morínigo's advisers confidently anticipated a favorable United States response, having been assured by Sumner Welles at Rio that any "request of the Paraguayan Government" for development assistance would receive the Roosevelt administration's "most favorable consideration." Nevertheless, when the actual Paraguayan aid request arrived in Washington, it evoked a negative reaction. "Such a program would be quite out of the question." the State Department's Emilio Collado advised Welles. "There is absolutely no possibility that the loan could be serviced," nor would it be possible to supply the rather large amounts of machinery" needed for new industries during the midst of a world war. For their part, Export-Import Bank officials were skeptical that the Paraguayans were capable of carrying out a large-scale development program and concluded that, in general, "economic development in Paraguay" was "hopeless."[2]

Within a month, however, political developments in Paraguay had forced a complete reversal in U.S. attitudes. Throughout the first quarter of 1942, as Axis military victories in Europe and Asia continued unabated and U.S. military and economic aid to Paraguay failed to materialize, the numerous pro-Axis nationalists among Morínigo's military supporters grew increasingly disenchanted with the regime's decision to support the United States at the Rio Conference. By April, a bitter new foreign-policy debate was under way between the regime's military and civilian factions, with the powerful Frente de guerra officer group charging that as a result of poor judgment by Foreign Minister Argaña and his Tiempista colleagues, Paraguay was backing the wrong side in the war. On April 10, United States ambassador Wesley Frost informed the State Department that "Paraguay's rupture of relations with the Axis Powers was almost openly based upon the argument that this action would bring about economic and defense assistance from the United States" and that "the leaders in the movement for the rupture, Dr. Argaña and his friends, are now in danger of being retired from their positions because of the failure of this policy to secure results." Unless the United States at once granted "two or three substantial items" in the recent Paraguayan aid request "without investigation or cavil," Frost warned, "we shall in short order have our first defection from the eighteen nations which pledged support at Rio."[3]

In the meantime, however, the State Department had added new fuel to the fire by dispatching special emissary Avra Warren to Asunción to secure the removal of all Axis diplomatic representatives and Nazi agents from Paraguay in accordance with Rio Conference resolutions. After two days of "direct and sharp pressure" by Warren, Morínigo agreed to expel the Axis diplomats, and the decision immediately precipitated a crisis within the government. At a stormy cabinet meeting on May 1, the military faction condemned the United States' "persecution of peaceful Germans" in Paraguay, furiously rejected any move to expel Nazi agents from the country, and instead demanded Argaña's resignation, charging that the foreign minister had "tricked Paraguay with illusory promises of help which the United States will not make good." "Argaña's assurances in government circles after Rio that you promised him $7,000,000," Frost telegraphed Welles, "have now flared back badly. . . . Word has twice reached me that police-army fanatics . . . are resolute to reverse Paraguay's course and actually have plans to assassinate Argaña, Andrada, and myself." Argaña, Frost continued, "has withdrawn to his *estancia* to await your proposals." Forty-eight hours later, the State Department announced a large-scale program of United States assistance for economic development in Paraguay. The announcement, Frost reported, "saved the situation," silencing the pro-Axis military group at least temporarily.[4]

As part of its new assistance package, the Roosevelt administration agreed to launch a series of cooperative agricultural and health programs in Paraguay, supplying technical advisers and establishing regional hospitals and model training farms throughout the country. The heart of the U.S. aid program, however, was a grant of $3 million in Export-Import Bank credits for "public works, agricultural and industrial development projects." Nevertheless, the Paraguayans were soon to learn that the Roosevelt administration's perception of economic development in

Paraguay differed considerably from their own. For when Morínigo proposed to divide the $3 million in development credits evenly between processing industries and new highways, he immediately discovered that neither the Export-Import Bank nor the State Department showed any enthusiasm for Paraguayan industrialization projects and that, instead, U.S. officials were interested only in additional highway construction that would utilize the New York–based engineering firm already employed in Paraguay under the United States' 1939 highway credit to Estigarribia.[5] The Export-Import Bank immediately informed Morínigo's representatives that "the three million dollars should be used for roads," and began to discuss terms "in a manner which the Paraguayans did not like." When a perplexed Ambassador Frost complained to the State Department about the Export-Import Bank's "stubborn antagonism" toward "productive industries" in Paraguay, Export-Import Bank president Pierson responded: "We have had occasion during the past several years to study Paraguay's economic problems. We do not think they will be solved by any considerable development of greater amounts of exportable products or the increased local manufacture of products hitherto imported." "Any public works which are carried out now," Pierson concluded, "will have to be confined largely to simple highway construction." "Your comments," the State Department assured Pierson, "are in accord with [our] own understanding." Lacking alternatives, Morínigo reluctantly accepted the bank's dictates and agreed to allocate an initial $2 million of the new development credit to highway construction.[6]

The Paraguayans nevertheless persisted in their efforts to secure U.S. aid for industrial development. During a June 1943 state visit to the United States, Morínigo and his advisers requested authorization to apply the remaining $1 million of the $3 million development credit to industrialization projects, submitting proposals for textile mills; dehydrated-milk and citrus-concentrates industries; cement, jute, and mandioca starch plants; and refrigerated agricultural warehouses. The initial U.S. response was encouraging. State Department officials assured the Paraguayans that U.S. industrial experts would be sent to Paraguay at once to study the feasibility of such projects, while Roosevelt personally expressed enthusiasm for Paraguayan processing industries in his conversations with Morínigo. Again, however, the Paraguayans were to be disappointed. The industrial experts promised by the State Department failed to arrive, and the Export-Import Bank continued to adopt a hostile attitude toward all development projects other than highway construction. "The Paraguayans feel that they are being given the run-around," Frost told the United States ambassador to Argentina in September 1943. "The Paraguayans feel that their roads will not be enough

77

unless they have new production and new markets." "From my standpoint," Frost added confidentially, "the great worry is whether those who

Higinio Morínigo and his advisers at Blair House during 1943 state visit to the
United States. *From left to right:* Foreign Minister Luis Argaña, Morínigo,
Finance Minister Rogelio Espinoza, First Cavalry Division Commander Victori-
ano Benítez Vera. (Courtesy of the National Geographic Society.)

direct financial operations in the Department will continue in their positions and in their attitude opposing Paraguay's real needs."[7]

If the Roosevelt administration seemed reluctant to assist Morínigo in his industrial-development program, it was considerably less averse to aiding United States private industry to expand into Paraguay. During Morínigo's 1943 state visit to the United States, the State Department arranged for the Paraguayan leader to be entertained by officials of International Business Machines Corporation, General Motors, and other major representatives of U.S. corporate enterprise. Meanwhile, the State Department was actively promoting the commercial penetration of Paraguay by the U.S. aviation, telecommunications, and petroleum industries —three industrial sectors crucial to the expanding geopolitical and economic global interests of the United States during and after World War II.

In November 1940, the Roosevelt administration and Pan American Airways had established a secret "Airport Development Program," in

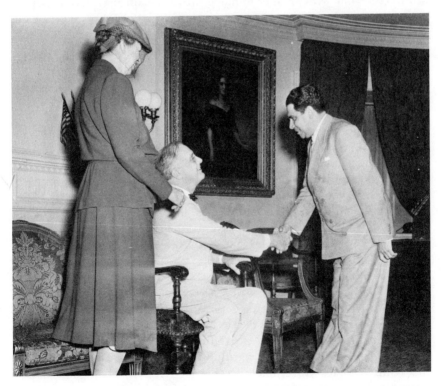

FDR and Eleanor Roosevelt greet Morínigo at the White House on 9 June 1943. (Courtesy of Wide World Photos.)

which Pan American—ostensibly on its own initiative but secretly utilizing government funds—undertook to construct modern airport facilities throughout Latin America. The program had both commercial and strategic motives. In negotiating airport-construction contracts with Latin American governments, Pan American—the "aerial ambassador of American industry," as the company referred to itself—was to seek special operating concessions for United States commercial airlines, thereby gaining a competitive advantage for U.S. air carriers over their European rivals in the Latin American aviation market. In addition, emergency landing rights at the projected airports were to be secured for United States military aircraft in the event that hemispheric defense operations became necessary. "Airfields throughout South America," program director George Marshall had said, "are an asset to us for military use and for future trade relations. . . . A great deal of money had better be concentrated to develop airfields all over the place."[8]

By early 1942, Pan American representatives had approached the Morínigo regime with an offer to modernize the main Paraguayan airport at Campo Grande, adjacent to Asunción's principal military and air base. As negotiations progressed, however, the State Department suddenly discovered that the airline's representatives were independently attempting to gain a 30-year monopoly for Pan American Airways over all commercial operations at the airport. Interceding in the matter, an irritated Roosevelt administration quickly forced Pan American to replace the monopoly-granting clause in its proposed contract with one that would grant free use of the airport to all aircraft "belonging to, registered in, operating for, or authorized by the United States."[9]

Morínigo, unable to resist such an unexpected opportunity to acquire a modern airport for Paraguay at no cost to his regime, eventually accepted the revised Pan American offer in July 1942. Nevertheless, many of his nationalistic military supporters had vehemently opposed the airport contract, viewing it as an unwarranted military and commercial concession to a foreign power and as a beachhead for United States "imperialism" in Paraguay. As a result, when Pan American engineers arrived at Campo Grande in August 1942 to survey the airfield, Colonel Benítez Vera and a group of cavalry officers stationed at the military base forcibly drove them away, firing several shots at the Americans as they fled. The incident—symbolic of the bitterness with which Latin American nationalists reacted to an expanding United States presence in the hemisphere—evoked a muted warning from the State Department that the "United States Government" considered it "in the highest degree important" that the airport be completed, and an embarrassed Morínigo subsequently promised to "keep the Cavalry at bay."[10]

During 1944, as modernization of the airport neared completion, officials of Pan American and Trans-World Airlines, backed by the State Department, approached Morínigo with proposals to establish a domestic commercial air service in Paraguay. The U.S. initiatives, however, conflicted with air-force commander in chief Pablo Stagni's plans to create a state-run national airline utilizing Paraguayan air-force personnel and lend-lease aircraft, and Stagni was able to forestall U.S. expansion into the domestic Paraguayan aviation market, at least for the time being.[11]

During his 1943 state visit, Morínigo had attempted to enlist the aid of the United States government in carrying out a petroleum survey of Paraguay. The Roosevelt administration, however, was hesitant to commit itself to a public program of overseas oil exploration and suggested that Paraguay should instead utilize the services of a private United States oil company. Almost immediately, Morínigo was contacted by representatives of the Union Oil Company of California, and by early 1944, Union Oil officials were in Asunción, endeavoring to negotiate an oil-exploration contract and hinting privately that if their proposal were accepted, "various members of the [Morínigo] regime . . . would be given employment" by the company. Meanwhile, however, Standard Oil of New Jersey and Socony had also begun to express interest in Paraguay's potential petroleum reserves, and when it became known that Union Oil was seeking exclusive 10-year exploration and exploitation rights in the Paraguayan Chaco, the State Department registered its sharp opposition to the "strong monopolistic provisions" of the Union Oil proposal, instructing Ambassador Frost to point out to the Paraguayan government "that the proposal closes the door to entrance into Paraguay by other interests" and to inform "the appropriate authorities" of the State Department's "sincere hope that the contract will not be monopolistic." "It is desirable that *an* American interest get a foothold in Paraguay," the State Department noted. "We have no particular interest in which American oil interest makes a deal with the Paraguayans. However . . . , it is incumbent on us to go as far as we can to avoid the perpetration of a monopoly." Duly admonished, Union Oil quickly abandoned its efforts to secure a monopoly, and aided by "splendid assistance from the American Embassy at Asunción," it successfully concluded a petroleum agreement with Morínigo in October 1944. Company officials privately acknowledged that they had "made a pretty good deal," obtaining 35-year tax-free exploitation rights in the Chaco, with royalty payments of only 12 percent to the Paraguayan government.[12]

Throughout the war, the Roosevelt administration also actively encouraged the International Telephone and Telegraph Corporation to expand its operations in Latin America, because, according to the State

Department, the company supplied a "needed part of our export trade and it was necessary to assure the predominance of American interests in the communication field as against any European interest." During 1942, in fact, I.T.&T. received Export-Import Bank credits to enlarge and modernize its Latin American facilities.[13] Thus, when the United States embassy in Asunción learned in October 1944 that Morínigo was contemplating the nationalization of Paraguay's German-owned telephone and radio-telecommunications systems,[14] it accordingly requested that the State Department "endeavor to interest" I.T.&T. in entering the Paraguayan market. Company officials, however, expressed concern that Morínigo might be planning to develop a state-owned telecommunications network. "I.T.&T.," they noted, "has no fear of competition from other private companies, but . . . it does fear government competition." Nevertheless, the company eventually decided, after prodding by the State Department, that while "from a commercial point of view, I.T.&T. is not particularly interested in expanding its operations in Paraguay . . . , from a policy point of view . . . it would be desirable for I.T.&T. to cooperate." And in June 1946, a year after Morínigo expropriated the German telecommunications company, I.T.&T. secured a contract to develop a modern domestic and international telecommunications system in Paraguay.[15]

Morínigo did not abandon his efforts to secure U.S. industrialization assistance, however. In early 1944 he announced plans to create a state development corporation to coordinate all economic-development activity in the country, and he requested that an industrial mission be sent from the United States to assist the new state agency in drawing up a comprehensive industrialization plan. Visiting Asunción in February 1944, John McClintock, executive secretary of the Inter-American Development Commission and assistant coordinator of Inter-American Affairs under Nelson Rockefeller, strongly advised the Paraguayans against a state-directed approach to development. "The development of the resources of Paraguay" could "best be attained through stability and sound economic policies which would encourage private enterprise," McClintock said, adding that if the Paraguayans ever hoped to encourage U.S. private enterprise to invest in their country, "the formation of such a corporation would be the best way" he "could think of to chill American interest." When Morínigo's advisers mentioned plans for the creation of hydroelectric power facilities to tap the energy resources of Paraguay's numerous rivers for industrial purposes, McClintock responded that "such a development at this stage of Paraguay's economic life was out of the question" and that "Paraguay should stick to charcoal and firewood until such new industries as might be developed had had a chance to demonstrate whether they were economic or not."[16]

Meanwhile, however, other United States officials in the field were painting an extremely positive picture of Paraguay's industrial potential. In October 1944, the Roosevelt administration finally agreed to send an industrial survey team to Paraguay. After studying the country for several months, the U.S. industrial experts reported that "good possibilities" existed for Paraguayan processing industries, particularly in the fields of lumber, leather goods, and vegetable oils. Simultaneously, United States agricultural experts in Paraguay were reporting that in view of the country's "potential agricultural wealth and . . . capacity to produce a wide range of food and fiber products . . . , industrial plans for Paraguay can be made with reasonable assurance of success." "Wonders can be achieved with Paraguay," the agricultural experts concluded. There were "dozens of types of industrial possibilities" if the country could

Wesley Frost. (Courtesy of the Oberlin College Archives.)

secure the "technical assistance and foreign capital" to develop them. "The economic toning-up of Paraguay," Ambassador Frost informed the State Department in mid 1944, "would . . . seem to depend upon . . . bringing into existence specialized industrial activities." If left to "private enterprise," Frost added, "the development of Paraguay will not advance rapidly or extensively." Nevertheless, no U.S. industrial aid was forthcoming. "The Department," Frost complained to a colleague, "has never admitted any interest except in roads and subsistence agriculture."[17]

By the time World War II neared its end, the Roosevelt administration had become increasingly indifferent to Morínigo's economic-development program. In late 1944, when the Paraguayans put forth yet another request for industrialization assistance, the United States commercial attaché in Asunción submitted a memorandum strongly opposing such aid:

> It is to be hoped [he wrote] that the United States Government will . . . diminish or discontinue rather than extend its functions in . . . those fields to which private enterprise can be better adapted. . . . The Government can do more in promoting trade, good will, and cultural interchange by attacking such problems as tariffs, port charges . . . , exchange controls, nationalistic laws . . . , etc., than it can by actively attempting to promote the commercial or industrial development of other countries. If these major obstacles are met by Government action, private enterprise will be free to undertake the development program.[18]

Not even the commercial attaché could foresee how energetically the United States would pursue precisely such a policy in the immediate postwar period.

7

Southeastern South America
and the
"American Century"

The United States emerged from World War II as the world's leading industrial power. Germany, Italy, and Japan now lay in ruins, doomed to inevitable defeat in an extended war by their insufficient reserves of manpower and raw materials.[1] Great Britain and the Soviet Union—the other leading industrial nations—had also suffered massive economic devastation during the war. For the United States, however, World War II had provided the long-sought cure for economic depression. Stimulated by huge wartime government contracts for military equipment and supplies, U.S. private industry made so dynamic a recovery that by 1945 the country was enjoying the highest levels of employment and national income in its history. And yet economic analysts were already warning that to maintain high industrial production and full employment in the postwar period, after federal military spending fell off and returning military forces reentered the civilian labor market, the nation would require substantially larger export markets to consume its industrial surpluses and that, within five years, annual exports of $10 billion would be needed to sustain domestic economic prosperity.[2] Accordingly, having reached the very zenith of its power and prestige in international affairs, the United States now directed its efforts toward forging a postwar international environment in which U.S. private enterprise would be free to develop the expanded foreign markets believed essential to continued U.S. economic vitality—an open world of international free trade, kept stable by a new United Nations international peacekeeping organization.[3]

During the war years, the United States had amassed an overwhelming preponderance of economic power in southeastern South America. By 1945, Germany's strong prewar economic position in the region had been totally destroyed, while British influence continued its steady

TABLE 6

Trade between Nations of Southeastern South America and Great Britain, Germany, and the United States, 1938 and 1946

	YEAR	TOTAL TRADE In Millions	TRADE WITH GREAT BRITAIN In Millions	TRADE WITH GREAT BRITAIN % of Total Trade	TRADE WITH GERMANY In Millions	TRADE WITH GERMANY % of Total Trade	TRADE WITH THE UNITED STATES In Millions	TRADE WITH THE UNITED STATES % of Total Trade
Argentina	1938	$ 837.398	$220.145	26.3	$ 91.907	11.0	$ 109.289	13.1
	1946	1,753.277	336.337	19.2	.721	0.0	340.162	19.4
Brazil	1938	590.882	56.541	9.6	130.224	22.0	173.028	29.3
	1946	1,650.445	139.114	8.4	.....		803.468	48.7
Paraguay	1938	14.550	1.637	11.3	1.858	12.8	1.578	10.8
	1946	48.238	4.696	9.7	.006	0.0	5.518	11.4
Uruguay	1938	123.227	28.707	23.3	24.482	19.9	9.647	7.8
	1946	299.917	47.134	15.7	.429	0.1	93.676	31.2
Region	1938	1,566.057	307.030	19.6	248.471	15.9	293.542	18.7
	1946	3,751.877	527.281	14.1	1.156	0.0	1,242.824	33.1

SOURCES: United States, Department of Commerce, *Foreign Commerce Yearbook, 1948* (Washington, D.C.: Government Printing Office, 1950), pp. 291, 383, 404; and ibid., *1949* (Washington, D.C.: Government Printing Office, 1951), p. 268.

erosion, leaving the United States virtually unchallenged as the region's dominant industrial trading partner. The total volume of United States trade with southeastern South America had increased by 323 percent during World War II, from less than $294 million in 1938 to more than $1.24 billion by 1946 (see table 6). At the same time, the United States' relative share of the region's foreign trade was expanding from less than 19 percent in 1938 to over 33 percent by 1946, while Great Britain's 19 percent of 1938 was decreasing to only 14 percent in 1946, and Germany's 1938 share of 16 percent was completely eliminated.

United States purchases of southeastern South America's export products increased by 358 percent during the war, due primarily to emergency stockpiling of strategic raw materials and foodstuffs for the United States' armed forces. As a result, the United States now replaced Great Britain as southeastern South America's principal customer, increasing its relative share of the region's export trade from 18 percent in 1938 to over 27 percent by 1946, while Britain's 1938 share of 23 percent fell to 16, and Germany's 16 percent of 1938 was lost completely (see table 7).

It was in the supply of manufactured imports, however, that U.S. economic power expanded most dramatically. A 292 percent increase in sales of U.S. goods in the region during the war raised the United States' relative share of the region's import market from 19 percent in 1938 to a commanding 43 percent by the end of the war. Great Britain's relative share, in the meantime, dropped from 16 percent to 10, while Germany's 1938 share of 16 percent was totally absorbed by U.S. interests (see table 8).

Paralleling the growth in trade was a sharp influx of private United States investment capital into the region. Throughout the war, the Roosevelt administration struggled to liquidate German "proclaimed list" firms operating in South America and to secure their markets for United States companies. As a special inducement to encourage United States private enterprise to expand southward into the vacuum left by retreating German capital, the administration in 1942 wrote into the Internal Revenue Code a Western Hemisphere Trade Corporations clause granting lower corporate income-tax rates to U.S. companies that undertook new operations in Latin America.[4] Encouraged, assisted, and occasionally prodded by the State Department, a wide variety of United States corporations—manufacturers of automobiles, electrical equipment, chemicals and pharmaceuticals, and processed foods—opened branch offices and plants in southeastern South America, usually establishing mixed multinational subsidiaries in partnership with local capital.[5] By the end of the war, the region's vital international commercial transportation and communications links with the rest of the world were dominated

TABLE 7

Exports from Nations of Southeastern South America to Great Britain, Germany, and the United States, 1938 and 1946

FROM	YEAR	TOTAL EXPORTS In Millions	EXPORTS TO GREAT BRITAIN In Millions	% of Total Exports	EXPORTS TO GERMANY In Millions	% of Total Exports	EXPORTS TO THE UNITED STATES In Millions	% of Total Exports
Argentina	1938	$ 409.212	$134.265	32.8	$ 47.788	11.7	$ 34.641	8.5
	1946	1,183.174	261.078	22.1	.683	0.1	177.529	15.0
Brazil	1938	295.558	25.915	8.8	56.348	19.1	101.458	34.3
	1946	980.745	85.866	8.8	.....	.....	413.892	42.2
Paraguay	1938	6.966	.907	13.0	.991	14.2	.852	12.2
	1946	26.754	3.093	11.6	.....	.....	1.030	3.8
Uruguay	1938	61.660	16.133	26.2	14.490	23.5	2.449	4.0
	1946	152.765	34.397	22.5	.429	0.3	45.538	29.8
Region	1938	773.396	177.220	22.9	119.617	15.5	139.400	18.0
	1946	2,343.438	384.434	16.4	1.112	0.0	637.989	27.2

Sources: United States, Department of Commerce, *Foreign Commerce Yearbook, 1948* (Washington, D.C.: Government Printing Office, 1950), pp. 291, 383, 404; and ibid., *1949* (Washington, D.C.: Government Printing Office, 1951), p. 268.

TABLE 8

IMPORTS BY NATIONS OF SOUTHEASTERN SOUTH AMERICA FROM GREAT BRITAIN, GERMANY, AND THE UNITED STATES, 1938 AND 1946

To	Year	TOTAL IMPORTS In Millions	IMPORTS FROM GREAT BRITAIN In Millions	% of Total Imports	IMPORTS FROM GERMANY In Millions	% of Total Imports	IMPORTS FROM THE UNITED STATES In Millions	% of Total Imports
Argentina	1938	$ 428.186	$ 85.880	20.1	$ 44.119	10.3	$ 74.648	17.4
	1946	570.103	75.259	13.2	.038	0.0	162.633	28.5
Brazil	1938	295.324	30.626	10.4	73.876	25.0	71.570	24.2
	1946	669.700	53.248	8.0	.....	.....	389.576	58.2
Paraguay	1938	7.584	.730	9.6	.867	11.4	.726	9.6
	1946	21.484	1.603	7.5	.006	0.0	4.488	20.9
Uruguay	1938	61.567	12.574	20.4	9.992	16.2	7.198	11.7
	1946	147.152	12.737	8.6	.....	.....	48.138	32.7
Region	1938	792.661	129.810	16.4	128.854	16.3	154.142	19.4
	1946	1,408.439	142.847	10.1	.044	0.0	604.835	42.9

SOURCES: United States, Department of Commerce, *Foreign Commerce Yearbook, 1948* (Washington, D.C.: Government Printing Office, 1950), pp. 291, 383, 404; and ibid., *1949* (Washington, D.C.: Government Printing Office, 1951), p. 268.

by U.S. firms—its commercial aviation by Pan American Airways and local Pan American subsidiaries, its merchant shipping by the Moore-McCormack Lines,[6] and its telecommunications systems by International Telephone and Telegraph. In addition, United States oil companies had become increasingly active in the region, lured by record rates of return on petroleum investments and vigorously supported by government officials concerned over the strategic and economic implications of a 38 percent increase in U.S. oil consumption during World War II (from 3.50 million barrels per day in 1938 to 4.85 million by 1945) that had transformed the United States from an oil-exporting nation to an oil importer.[7]

Although the expansion of United States economic influence in the region during the war had been formidable, the Roosevelt administration anticipated even greater gains in the postwar period. Throughout the war, U.S. planners eagerly looked forward to completing the consolidation of U.S. economic hegemony in the hemisphere after the war—convinced, in the words of Eric Johnston, president of the United States Chamber of Commerce and chairman of the United States section of the Inter-American Development Commission, that "just as the last century in Latin America was a 'British Century' the next would be an American Century."[8] Indeed, as early as June 1942, administration officials noted that "the vigor and confidence with which the Board of Economic Warfare had entered the field of postwar planning for Latin America had raised fears that the Board might transform the Good Neighbor Policy into a new type of imperialism."[9] Particularly exciting to wartime planners was the prospect of further massive increases in U.S. industrial exports to southeastern South America after the war. Recognizing that the United States would probably be the region's "only available source of supply of . . . capital goods" after the war, the Foreign Economic Administration predicted in 1944 that U.S. sales of "metals and manufactures, machinery and vehicles, chemicals and related products" during the first three postwar years would exceed prewar levels by 316 percent in Argentina, 530 percent in Paraguay, and 610 percent in Brazil. "In view of the need of Paraguay for the kind of goods to improve its economy . . . which probably only the United States can supply," the F.E.A. concluded, "we do not consider this increase to be unreasonably great."[10]

Buoyed by such tantalizing projections and finally free of German competition, the Roosevelt administration late in the war mounted a two-pronged attack against the last remaining impediment to U.S. economic expansion in the hemisphere: the rising tide of Latin American economic nationalism that had continued to gain momentum during

World War II. "The achievement of [a world economic] system of equal treatment and expansion," Assistant Secretary of State for Latin American Affairs Spruille Braden announced at the end of the war, "demands . . . a concerted effort to eliminate every form of economic discrimination," particularly "the virus of economic nationalism."[11] "The exaggerated nationalisms, now so prevalent everywhere," Braden asserted, "must be completely extirpated. . . . To eliminate those nationalisms . . . is our firm purpose."[12]

To extirpate economic nationalism in southeastern South America, the United States moved, in 1945, to forge a new political and economic climate in the region more conducive to unrestricted penetration by U.S. private enterprise. First, the United States government applied pressure on the region's leaders to adopt a more liberal economic approach toward international trade, economic development, and foreign investment, seeking, in the words of Secretary of State James F. Byrnes, to discourage "restrictive policies harmful to American commercial interests."[13] As the German strategic threat to the hemisphere subsided, the United States abruptly terminated its economic-assistance programs in the region. United States foreign aid was instead now urgently rechanneled toward Europe and Asia to combat the serious new strategic threat to U.S. global interests presented by an expansionistic Soviet Union as it suddenly moved into the postwar power vacuum on those continents.[14] The Latin Americans were now informed that in the future they must rely on private capital and foreign investment to finance their industrial-development programs and that to induce the private sector— domestic and foreign—to invest in industrialization projects, they would be well advised to eschew nationalistic and statist approaches and instead concentrate on creating an attractive internal investment climate free from inhibiting controls on private capitalists and foreign investors. "It must be recognized," Assistant Secretary of State Braden explained, "that the sound industrialization of a country can by all odds be carried out more effectively under the dynamic system of private and, where possible, competitive enterprise, to which we are dedicated, than it ever can by government. Just as the United States and European capital both greatly benefited from the latter's investments here, so less developed nations who desire to advance the rate of their economic growth may profit by encouraging the entry of capital from abroad."[15] It was unfortunate, Braden told the Chicago Executives' Club in 1946, that

> there has appeared a school of thought which, when considering United States cooperation in the development of Latin America, overlooks or even in a few cases condemns the use of private capital. Instead it advocates that the requisite financing be done by our government,

either in the form of loans at low rates of interest or of what is tanta-
mount to outright grants, in the case of certain public health, nutrition,
and educational projects. . . .

The institution of private property ranks with those of religion
and the family as a bulwark of civilization. To tamper with private
enterprise, except to apply well-conceived, legal, and essential controls,
will precipitate a disintegration of life and liberty as we conceive
and treasure them. . . .

The time has come to realize that the United States Treasury is
not an inexhaustible reservoir.[16]

At the same time, the elimination of German competition permitted the
United States to take a more aggressive stance against nationalistic trade
policies—the high tariffs, import quotas, exchange controls, and so forth,
which the Latin Americans were relying upon to protect and expand
their infant industries after the war. As a result, United States diplomats
were soon lobbying for the elimination of trade restrictions and attempting to negotiate "treaties of friendship, commerce, and navigation" that
guaranteed free trade and fair treatment for foreign capital.[17]

The changed tone in U.S. economic policy was revealed at the 1945
Inter-American Conference on Problems of War and Peace at Mexico
City. The Latin Americans arrived at the conference hoping to persuade
the United States to provide the necessary funds for a comprehensive
program of postwar economic development in the hemisphere, finding
low-interest U.S. public loans clearly preferable to the various alternative
mechanisms of development financing available to their governments:
high-interest loans from private lending institutions, private investment
by exploitative foreign capital, or any of the domestic revenue-raising
mechanisms that would require the governing elites to tax their own
wealth.[18] Latin American suggestions at Mexico City "that the American
nations approach, in . . . the TVA fashion, the economic problems of
the postwar," however, elicited only silence from United States representatives.[19] Instead, the U.S. delegation concentrated its efforts on draft-
ing an "Economic Charter of the Americas" that called for "expanding
domestic and foreign trade and investment," the reduction of trade barriers, "elimination of economic nationalism in all its forms," "just and
equitable treatment and encouragement for the enterprises, skills and
capital brought from one country to another," promotion of "the system
of private enterprise in production," and agreement "to refrain from the
establishment of state enterprises for the conduct of trade."[20]

Recalling the enthusiasm with which the United States had provided
development aid when Nazi Germany threatened U.S. interests in the
hemisphere, the Latin Americans desperately evoked the specter of a

new strategic threat to the hemisphere, warning the North Americans that the Soviet Union was now actively fomenting social revolution in their countries and that only massive U.S. economic aid would enable them to improve standards of living enough to fend off the imminent threat of Russian-manipulated Communist revolutions throughout the hemisphere.[21] Such a ploy, however, proved premature in 1945. The State Department had been warily on the alert against Russian penetration of Latin America for some time, instructing U.S. diplomatic missions in Latin America as early as December 1943 to report "any Soviet activities in the hemisphere . . . inimical to the security of the hemisphere, to its political or economic stability, or to our own interests."[22] Yet, while viewing "International Communism" as "the tool of the Kremlin, which the latter utilizes to advance Russian imperialistic designs . . . throughout the world," the State Department nevertheless saw no cause for alarm in Latin America during the early postwar period, judging the communist threat to be merely "a potential rather than an immediately serious one in Latin America."[23] Consequently, the United States delegation at Mexico City rebuffed all Latin American proposals for a United States–funded hemispheric development program and in the end managed to secure conference approval of its "Economic Charter of the Americas" virtually intact.[24]

The second main thrust of the United States attack on economic nationalism was a campaign of direct intervention in the internal politics of the nations of southeastern South America. During 1945, the State Department actively intervened in the domestic affairs of Argentina, Brazil, and Paraguay to remove from power the authoritarian nationalist sector of the dominant elite, whose nationalistic economic policies were so incompatible with United States economic interests, and to replace it with the traditional "liberal" sector, whose economic philosophy was more favorable to international free trade, a laissez-faire/private-enterprise approach to economic development, and an open door for foreign capital and who consequently could be expected to be more receptive to U.S. trade and investment. Indeed, just as the southward spread of U.S. economic hegemony in the Caribbean basin during the early years of the century had brought with it three decades of forceful United States interventionism in that region, so now the continued southward extension of U.S. economic predominance over southeastern South America during World War II was to bring in its wake deliberate, if considerably more subtle and less forceful, U.S. interventionism to restructure that region's political economy into a pattern more advantageous to United States interests.

Ostensibly, postwar political interventionism was motivated by the desire to cleanse southeastern South America of "fascist dictatorships" and restore democratic governments. It would appear, however, that practical economic considerations rather than idealistic ideological or political principles lay behind the State Department's new aggressiveness. Certainly any United States concern for democracy had been singularly absent during the war, when the German threat had prompted the State Department to cultivate close and friendly ties with Vargas and his corporatist dictatorship in Brazil and with Morínigo's nationalist revolutionary dictatorship in Paraguay. Nor did the past performance of the region's liberal elite provide any reason to realistically hope that that political element would pay more than the scantest lip service to the principles of representative democracy after the war. "The long-term defense of the United States," the Foreign Economic Administration concluded in December 1944, "requires that the soil and resources of the other American republics remain in friendly hands and that their policies be such as to assure . . . the continuation of . . . inter-American economic and political cooperation."[25] The State Department agreed. According to a representative of the Division of Brazilian Affairs in 1945, "our own welfare depends to a large extent on the soundness of economic conditions in this Hemisphere. We cannot dodge our responsibilities in this connection by hiding behind the nebulous curtain of 'non-intervention.' "[26]

Throughout southeastern South America by the end of the war, the forces of authoritarian nationalism were desperately attempting to protect their position in a rapidly changing international ideological environment. Fascism had by now been thoroughly discredited as a system of national development—its "high ideals" transformed into "tales of dread"[27] as the combination of coercive dictatorship and unrestrained nationalism degenerated horrifyingly in Germany into mass liquidation of suspect alien minority groups—and it had become increasingly evident that corporatist dictatorships would have no place in the new international order being organized by the victorious Allied powers. As a result, southeastern South America's authoritarian nationalists now swiftly adapted to the prevailing ideological currents of 1945 by shedding their authoritarian images, ostensibly embracing democratic principles, restoring political liberties, and making preparations for free elections. As the region's political systems reopened, the liberal elites immediately moved to reassert their supremacy, reactivating their traditional party organizations and preparing to regain power in the forthcoming elections. It soon became apparent, however, that the authoritarian nationalists intended to use democratic processes to maintain themselves in power and perpetuate an essentially corporatist and authoritarian nationalist direction in national policy under a façade of democratic institutions. During 1945, Vargas in Brazil, Perón in Argentina, and Morínigo in Paraguay were all attempting to build new power bases of popular electoral support among their lower-class majorities in preparation for their own emergence as "democratic" leaders, forging their own Labor parties from the ranks of their state-controlled trade-union movements and mobilizing mass political support with the emotional public rhetoric of populist nationalism—promising increased social welfare and material progress for the workers, national industrial self-sufficiency, and economic emancipation from imperialistic foreign capital and the *"vendepatria"* liberal oligarchy that collaborated with it.[28] As the liberal elites maneuvered to defeat their authoritarian nationalist rivals, they found the State Department to be a most helpful ally.

In Argentina in early 1945, the Farrell-Perón dictatorship expediently declared war on the besieged Axis powers and scheduled elections for February 1946. The United States responded by restoring diplomatic relations in April 1945. United States officials had been anxious to normalize relations with Argentina in order to include the latter in a cohesive hemispheric voting bloc at the forthcoming United Nations organizing conference at San Francisco, convinced that unless they "operated with a solid group in this hemisphere" they "could not do what we wanted to do on the world front."[29] Yet normalization of relations did not imply any United States desire for a rapprochement with Farrell and Perón, for one month after recognizing their government, the State Department appointed Spruille Braden as ambassador to Argentina and launched a belligerent "crack-down policy"[30] to undermine their regime and defeat Perón's populist campaign for the presidency in the 1946 election.

Arriving in Buenos Aires, Braden found Perón to be the "embodiment of . . . Fascist military control," and he warned Washington that "British and American trade and investments in this country . . . may be rendered valueless by continuance of present type of govt. Perón is on record as intending to recover Argentine patrimony from foreign malefactors."[31] As ambassador, Braden immediately made himself a rallying point for opposition forces in Argentine politics, publicly attacking the regime in speeches throughout the country, transforming the United States embassy into a meeting place for anti-Peronist politicians, and working closely with representatives of Argentina's traditional political parties to help them devise an effective strategy against Perón.[32]

Rewarded for his efforts by promotion to assistant secretary of state for Latin American affairs, Braden returned to the United States in September 1945, pledging to continue his fight on behalf of "the democratic elements in Argentina."[33] Soon, however, embassy officials in Buenos Aires began to question the wisdom of such an approach. Perón, Chargé d'Affaires John Cabot informed Washington, represented a "fairly long step forward toward social revolution in Argentina," and the effect of his "social measures will probably leave their mark on Argentine social thinking for years." Although it was a "tragedy," wrote Cabot, that it had been left to "a Fascist dictator" to implement needed social and economic reforms, "the people most vociferous in the opposition were by no means notable for their democratic leanings three years ago— quite the contrary, it was they who were largely responsible, by their reactionary policies, for the present mess here." By continuing to support the latter against Perón, Cabot concluded, "I can see danger that we shall not only be accused of blocking social reform but, worse, that we shall be charged with the worst sort of dollar diplomacy to protect our capital from the legitimate demands of Argentine labor." "[The real] choice is probably Perón or chaos rather than Perón or democracy."[34]

Nevertheless, in Washington, Braden was at work on a diplomatic "atomic bomb" to destroy Perón's campaign—a catalog of material compiled from captured German documents to show that Perón and his colleagues had collaborated with Nazi Germany during the war, material that would add fuel to the anti-Peronist opposition's campaign charges that he was a fascist. Although State Department officials cautioned that the available evidence did not constitute "a good court case" against Perón, and despite warnings from Cabot in Buenos Aires that release of the material would be regarded in Argentina as a "clumsy effort to influence [the] election and consequently as further alleged intervention in Argentine internal affairs," Braden published the so-called Blue Book twelve days before the election, hoping that its disclosures would do irreparable damage to Perón's reputation in the last critical days of the campaign.[35]

In the meantime, a more subtle form of United States intervention was taking place in Brazil. In early 1945, Getúlio Vargas announced that new elections would be held in December and that he would retire from office at that time. In the ensuing political campaign, the Brazilian elite quickly coalesced into two new political parties and put forth air-force General Eduardo Gomes and War Minister Eurico Dutra as candidates for the presidency. Despite his avowed intention to retire, however, Vargas was soon suspiciously cultivating Brazil's urban workers with populist rhetoric and paternalistic social welfarism, and the appearance in August 1945 of a "spontaneous" public campaign by Vargas's supporters calling on the dictator to postpone elections and continue in office raised widespread suspicion that he would soon claim a popular mandate to remain as president without elections and carry out an internal coup d'état similar to that which had preserved him in power in 1937.[36]

The possibility that Vargas might somehow circumvent the scheduled elections and remain in power was a source of growing concern to the United States. From the U.S. perspective, both Gomes and Dutra were perfectly acceptable presidential candidates. Gomes and his supporters publicly advocated a return to liberal economic policies, a relaxation of state controls and protective tariffs, and "the collaboration of foreign capital" and were, according to a State Department analysis, "very friendly to the United States so that any government which they headed might be expected to continue satisfactory cooperation with us." Dutra, the former authoritarian nationalist now turned "ardent democrat," was publicly pledging himself to "strong and indestructible ties of friendship" between Brazil and the United States and was calling for continued collaboration "without restrictions."[37] Vargas, on the other hand, was becoming an increasing irritant to United States economic interests in Brazil in 1945 as he enhanced his populist image with a spate of nationalistic new decree-laws restricting foreign imports, subjecting foreign enterprises to strict regulation, and banning foreign capital from participation in the development of a Brazilian oil-refining industry.[38]

As signs of an impending internal coup by Vargas continued to mount, the State Department decided to apply public pressure on his regime to hold elections as scheduled.[39] The U.S. ambassador in Brazil, Adolf Berle, analyzed the situation in mid September. "Elections," he wrote, "mean a politically conservative and economically reactionary candidate—either Gomes or Dutra would be that—under the form of democracy," while "perpetuation of the dictatorship means absence of democracy, a popular President with the support of the masses, and probably an Army revolt." Although Berle recognized that "to declare against continuance of the dictatorship . . . probably prevents any immediate progress towards much-needed economic reform," he concluded that "we had best ask for democracy and get it."[40] Nine days later, after conferring in Rio with Spruille Braden as the latter was returning from Buenos Aires to Washington to become assistant secretary of state, Berle delivered a widely publicized speech to Brazilian journalists, in which he publicly expressed the United States' "confidence" that the Vargas government, "whose word the United States has always found inviolable," would respect its "solemn promise of free elections in Brazil."[41] A month later, the Brazilian army, eager for Brazil to play a major role in postwar world affairs in close partnership with the United States and fearing that Vargas's political mobilization of the working classes might threaten its own political position and the traditional social structure, quietly removed Vargas from office.[42]

Political intervention produced mixed results for United States economic interests in southeastern South America during the early postwar period. In Argentina, Braden's belligerent tactics gave Perón a valuable opportunity to portray himself as the defender of Argentina's sovereignty against the forces of U.S. imperialism and their Argentine collaborators. Sweeping to victory in the 1946 election, Perón immediately launched a nationalistic economic program to achieve "the economic independence of Argentina," buying out several key foreign-owned industries (including the nation's railroad and telephone systems and several other public utilities) and placing Argentina's foreign commerce under the control of a state trading agency designed to reduce Argentina's dependence on foreign industrial imports.[43]

More satisfactory circumstances resulted in Brazil. After the overthrow of Vargas, elections were held in December 1945 as scheduled, and the victor, Dutra, immediately reinstituted laissez-faire, free-enterprise economic policies favorable to United States interests—dismantling the *Estado novo*'s state controls, reconcentrating Brazil's "essentially . . . agrarian" economy on "the export of primary products and foodstuffs" and "the import of . . . manufactured goods and processed foodstuffs," and offering an open door to foreign investors and traders.[44]

A third episode of U.S. interventionism had also taken place in southeastern South America, however. The State Department intervened to restore "democracy" in Paraguay at the end of the war, with consequences that were to have a profound impact on the contours of Paraguayan politics for at least the next three decades.

8

The United States and the
Restoration of "Democracy"
in Paraguay

Throughout World War II, the Morínigo regime had continued to base its foreign policy on a carefully calculated opportunism. While officially aligning Paraguay with the Allies as an "associated nation," Morínigo simultaneously safeguarded his position with the Axis by simply ignoring all international commitments to restrict Axis activities in his country. The populous German immigrant communities and extensive Nazi organizational network in Paraguay remained free from government controls throughout the war, and Morínigo consistently rejected the United States' repeated complaints against the widespread Nazi presence in Paraguay as constituting unwarranted foreign interference in his nation's internal affairs. He also nationalistically reaffirmed his economic independence by refusing to recognize either the United States' "proclaimed list" or the British "black list" during the war and persistently awarded government contracts to local Axis business firms. Meanwhile, Nazi agents in Morínigo's secret police and Paraguay's German-owned telephone system tapped the telephone communications of the United States and British embassies in Asunción, while aided by Morínigo's air-force commander in chief, Colonel Pablo Stagni, and other pro-Axis government officials, German agents passed freely through Paraguay along a South American "underground railroad," relaying espionage information and smuggling platinum, industrial diamonds, and other strategic materials out to coastal areas. By 1944, United States officials were expressing concern that Morínigo would permit Paraguay to become "a refuge for dangerous Axis nationals" after the war.[1]

By early 1943, however, the Allied invasion of North Africa and U.S. naval successes in the Pacific had finally reversed the unbroken string of Axis military advances, and Morínigo's international posture promptly began to shift accordingly. Throughout 1943 and 1944, as the momentum of the war turned inexorably in favor of the Allies and the likelihood of eventual Axis defeat became ever more apparent, he took steps to strengthen his government's standing in the Allied camp, informing his authoritarian supporters in October 1943 that since the postwar period would probably be dominated by the Anglo-American democracies, it behooved Paraguay to make a few appropriate "gestures" in order not to remain outside the "democratic current" that could be expected to prevail in world affairs after the war.[2]

As an initial gesture, Morínigo softened his antidemocratic image and strengthened his constitutional legitimacy by having himself "elected" to a full five-year term as president in a rigorously controlled 1943 election. A careful copy of preceding Colorado and Liberal presidential elections, the 1943 "plebiscite" admirably demonstrated the cold realities of Paraguayan "democracy" in action. To assure an impressive voter turnout, the election was preceded by an official announcement that voting was compulsory and that any eligible voter who failed to participate would be subject to a 500-peso fine. On election day, all Paraguayan adult males[3] thus dutifully reported to their designated polling places. Entering a room decorated with posters instructing them to "Vote for General Higinio Morínigo," the voters presented themselves before a public ballot box presided over by a delegation of government election officials. There they surrendered their identification papers, which the election officials utilized to record each voter's identity on his respective ballot slip—thereby eliminating the risks of a secret ballot. The printed ballots read simply "I vote for Higinio Morínigo for the 1943–1948 presidential term." If the voter approved of the incumbent candidate and chose to remain in good standing with the regime, he deposited his ballot in the box. If he wished to assert his independence and vote for someone else, he was required to cross out Morínigo's name and write in an alternate choice—in full view of the watchful election officials. Predictably, the final election returns gave Morínigo a landslide victory of some 170,000 affirmative votes to 11,000 "blank ballots," totals that closely approximated Estigarribia's 1939 presidential "election."[4]

Other gestures followed, paralleling the course of the war. In April 1943, Morínigo finally terminated the contract of Paraguay's pro-Axis Vichy French military mission and accepted the Roosevelt administration's offer to provide United States military advisers. By mid 1943, the editorial tone of the government-controlled Paraguayan press had conspicuously begun to shed its former pro-Axis/antidemocracy orientation in favor of a pro–United States/anticommunist point of view. Expediently shelving its campaign against liberalism, the regime now suddenly redirected its vituperations toward the evils of communism, with a press offensive reaching such intensity that film footage of Russian soldiers was censored out of all Allied propaganda newsreels shown in Asunción. During mid 1944, with the outcome of the war no longer in serious doubt, Morínigo imposed the first limited restrictions on a token number of Nazi agents in Paraguay. In February 1945—two months before Germany's capitulation—he opportunistically declared war on the Axis, in order to assure Paraguay's membership in the nascent United Nations organization and to establish eligibility for an eventual $5.5 million in Paraguayan war-indemnity claims against the defeated Axis. Not until May 1946, however, a year after the European war had ended, were Paraguay's local Nazi party and Nazi-controlled German schools and societies placed under effective governmental control.[5]

To preserve the façade of hemispheric solidarity, the Roosevelt administration patiently tolerated, and, in fact, continued to cultivate, Morínigo until the final year of the war. Then, in August 1944, two months after the successful Allied invasion of western Europe that placed the Third Reich on the road to final defeat, the State Department suddenly launched a diplomatic offensive against authoritarian nationalism in Paraguay, sending an aggressive new United States ambassador to Asunción and applying intense pressure on Morínigo to restore political liberties, hold new elections, and democratize Paraguay.

Opposing the sudden shift in United States policy, outgoing Ambassador Frost cautioned the State Department against interfering in Paraguayan domestic politics. As for Morínigo, Frost reported: "Few dictators in Latin America have been guilty of less violence than he. There have been no executions, no more exiling than in previous times, and as little imprisonment and violence as was consistent with remaining in power. I have known of far harsher methods not only in Brazil but in Chile. Comparatively speaking he may be regarded as a 'white-glove dictator.' "[6] The "pleasantest feature" of Morínigo's "Nationalist Revolution," Frost continued, was

> its devoted insistence upon honesty and good character on the part of all persons connected with the Government. This Embassy has maintained close contacts with all branches of the Government and has never had an instance in which corruption has been perceivable. . . . There has . . . been a surprisingly high record of patriotic public service. . . . Originating in bona fide indignation at previous political corruption, the Revolution's obsession with purity of government has been built up into a main asset in its political stock-in-trade. . . . Exceptions and flaws exist, but I have personally never seen any government in any country which came more nearly to deserving to be known as Spartan in its principles and conduct.[7]

On the other hand, Frost informed Washington, the prospect for "any genuine or thorough-going democratization" in Paraguay was "exceedingly improbable," and any effort "to restore democracy . . . would be rather ineffective." Democracy, he warned, "has never effectively operated here," and "no election has ever resulted in upsetting the group in power when it was held." "*Any* government which replaced Morínigo would within three months be as dictatorial as his." "The Colorados would rigidly exclude from office all but their own adherents; and the same is true of the Franquistas [Febreristas]. The Liberals . . . too would be forced to rest upon an army base, with resort to exiling and repression to no small extent. . . . They desire a return to a businessman's government."[8]

Arriving in Asunción, incoming Ambassador Willard Beaulac soon confirmed Frost's observations. Although Morínigo's government was "not the kind of regime we like," Beaulac reported, it had brought "considerable progress" to Paraguay and had accomplished "more than its predecessors did" in "road construction, agricultural training and development, public education, and public health." In fact, observed Beaulac, "a considerable portion of the Paraguayan populace is grateful for the material improvements made in the country by the regime," and "if an effort were made to organize and lead these people, the regime might . . . obtain substantial civilian support for itself." As for democracy, Beaulac acknowledged that it had never functioned in Paraguay and that under earlier Colorado and Liberal administrations, "government by martial law came very close to being the rule." "This sad little country has never had democracy," he wrote. "Free elections are unknown. . . . The 'outs' are traditionally 'democrats' and the 'ins' are traditionally 'despots.'" Moreover, Morínigo's "withering criticism and condemnation" of Paraguay's political parties for malfeasance in office was, the new ambassador admitted, "doubtless true." "I am skeptical that [Morínigo] will go very far . . . in the direction of democracy," he concluded, "but I am skeptical that any other group would do any better now."[9]

Nevertheless, with the full support and encouragement of the State Department, Beaulac immediately undertook a relentless personal campaign "to encourage democracy . . . and liberal institutions in Paraguay." Beginning in late 1944, he delivered "a number of forthright pro-democratic speeches" throughout the country. Carefully selecting his time and place so that Morínigo and his cabinet would be present, the ambassador pointedly warned his audiences that in "the unending war against tyranny and for democracy throughout the world," nations would be classified in two categories—"cooperative or uncooperative"—and that those which chose to remain uncooperative in the postwar period could expect to be dealt with accordingly by the victorious Allies.[10] "As I had anticipated," Beaulac informed Washington in September 1945, "these speeches . . . have been seized upon by the opposition as indicating American dissatisfaction with the regime."[11]

Beaulac also adopted a hard line in his private discussions with key governmental officials, taking advantage of every opportunity to lecture Morínigo and his advisers on the need for "press freedom, restitution of civil rights, and democratization." Pressing the regime to lift its four-year-old ban on political-party activities and hold "free and orderly elections," he bluntly informed the Paraguayans that the future availability of United States foreign aid for economic-development projects in Paraguay would be determined by "the degree of evolution toward Liberal, democratic government in Paraguay." Beaulac reserved his sternest tone for Morínigo personally, warning the president in December 1945 that further U.S. aid "would be related to the progressive democratization of Paraguay" and that "failure to correct the present situation would oblige our Government to withdraw the voluntary cooperation now being given to Paraguay and to refrain from giving additional cooperation."[12]

Threatened with the loss of his only available source of foreign aid for economic development, Morínigo struggled to find a formula that would satisfy the United States' sudden obsession with liberalization without dangerously undermining his own political power. In a new gesture toward democratization, he began, in late 1944, to display an uncharacteristic tolerance toward political dissent in Paraguay by permitting opposition political groups to hold their first public meetings in four years and maintaining a sullen silence as their spokesmen publicly attacked the dictatorship, demanded new elections, and called on the regime to convene a constituent assembly that would replace the authoritarian 1940 constitution with a liberal constitution modeled on that of 1870. Simultaneously, Morínigo turned his attention to the construction of an electoral power base for the regime, appointing as director of the Department of Labor an official known to be popular with Paraguay's trade unions and granting other favors calculated to guarantee the loyalty of organized labor. By 1945, plans were under way for the creation of an official Labor party. Such efforts were abruptly terminated, however, when Morínigo's authoritarian nationalist military supporters from the Frente de guerra lodge registered their vehement opposition. Intransigent in their hostility to all political parties and unwilling to share power with a potentially powerful labor movement, the Frente de guerra officers adamantly opposed any liberalization of the government and exhorted their leader not to abandon the nationalist revolution's authoritarian ideals in the face of United States pressure.[13]

Nevertheless, in January 1946, as Beaulac's warnings intensified and U.S. funds for economic-assistance projects in Paraguay began to run out, Morínigo informed the armed-forces officer corps that "foreign pressure" had become "too strong to resist" and that the nationalist revolution would now have to move into a democratic "second stage." Overriding the heated protests of his authoritarian military colleagues, he thereupon publicly announced a "three-point democratization program" for 1946, pledging to restore press freedom and political liberties in the near future and indicating that "preparations" would soon be undertaken for the election of a legislative chamber of deputies. Gratified, the United States quickly extended the funding of its cooperative agricultural-

Willard Beaulac. (Courtesy of the United States Department of State.)

assistance program in Paraguay for an additional eighteen months and hinted that further aid programs might well be forthcoming "after positive steps toward democratization had been taken."[14]

Morínigo's decision to liberalize his government set in motion a rapidly evolving chain of events that soon plunged Paraguay into chaos and bloodshed. In June 1946, when the Frente de guerra nationalists continued to stubbornly impede liberalization, Morínigo unexpectedly ousted them from their strategic commands and sent them into exile. Reaffirming his intention to "proceed with the program of democratization," he immediately abolished all press restrictions, restored political liberties to Paraguay's political parties, issued a general amnesty to all exiled political leaders, and scheduled congressional elections for the following year. Having cut himself adrift from his authoritarian power base, he now maneuvered to attach himself to a new prop of support that might keep him afloat in the changing postwar political currents. In July, he suddenly brought three Febreristas and three Colorados into his cabinet and formed a coalition government, apparently hoping to gradually subvert one or both of those parties to his own personal control and thereby capture a new power base with which to maintain himself in office. Paraguay's political parties had other ideas, however. To them, the startling political changes of 1946 signified the long-awaited weakening of Morínigo's hold on power, and in late July, the Liberals, Colorados, Febreristas, and Communists celebrated the promising new political climate at a joint public rally in Asunción's main plaza. "The dictator is no longer dictator," a Colorado speaker told the jubilant crowd; "the dictator is the prisoner of a democratic cabinet."[15]

It quickly became apparent, however, that the reopening of the Paraguayan political system had not opened the way for a new era of democratic politics in Paraguay. Rather than engaging in electoral preparations or a substantive debate of national issues, Paraguay's political parties instead concentrated on mobilizing their respective forces in a power struggle to seize the government and monopolize the perquisites of office. The Liberals responded to the loosening of political controls by actively smuggling arms into the country in preparation for a coup d'état, while the Communists celebrated their new political freedom by publicly threatening to hang Morínigo from a lamppost. Inside Morínigo's new coalition government, bitter political infighting immediately erupted as both the Febrerista and Colorado factions maneuvered to gain a position of dominance. Each faction quickly monopolized the cabinet ministries under its direction by summarily discharging all incumbent civil servants and replacing them with loyal party members. The Febreristas used their control of the Ministry of Agriculture and the Department of Labor to openly proselytize among Paraguay's lower classes, handing out free plows to rural peasants and free cake to Asunción workers, granting large-scale wage increases to members of pro-Febrerista labor unions, and settling strikes in favor of unions that agreed to affiliate with the party. Meanwhile, armed units of civilian Colorado militia ominously began to appear in Asunción's streets. Below the surface, Colorado, Febrerista, Liberal, and Communist leaders were all working furiously to win support from key military officers in anticipation of eventual coup attempts.[16]

In early January 1947, the Febreristas precipitated a governmental crisis by demanding majority representation in the cabinet and seeking guarantees that neither party in the coalition would accept Morínigo as a candidate for reelection at the end of his official term in 1948. The Febreristas' power play only served to push Morínigo and the Colorados closer together, however. On the night of 12 January 1947, army units loyal to Morínigo moved into Asunción and, working in close conjunction with several thousand mounted Colorado volunteers and pro-Colorado military and police elements, took up strategic positions throughout the capital, placed the leading Febrerista officials under arrest, and effectively seized control of the government. The following day, a new, all-Colorado cabinet was formed. Suddenly, for the first time since 1904, Paraguay again had a Colorado government, with the dexterous Morínigo remaining in power as president.[17]

The United States viewed the dramatic transformation of Morínigo's government in 1946 and early 1947 with considerable satisfaction. The expulsion of the Frente de guerra nationalists in June 1946 was particularly welcomed by U.S. officials. Upon learning of the ouster of air-force commander Stagni and his colleagues, the State Department immediately informed Pan American, Braniff, and other U.S. commercial airlines that the "difficulties which previously interfered with the assistance of United States air transportation companies in developing civilian aviation in Paraguay have now been removed."[18] Morínigo's subsequent decision to form a coalition government was hailed in Washington as having moved "the process of democratization . . . prodigiously forward." Nevertheless, U.S. officials made sharp distinctions in their appraisal of the two political parties making up the new coalition. The Febreristas were generally considered to be "young demagogic totalitarians," "wildmen," and "social dreamers" who "tended toward extreme socialism—even Communism." When the Febreristas, as part of their effort to cultivate lower-class popularity, enacted a party resolution that prohibited Febrerista lawyers from defending landowners or employers in disputes with tenants or workers, Ambassador Beaulac condemned the

106

action as "demagogy" and bluntly warned Febrerista cabinet ministers that he "could not recommend any investment in Paraguay by my government or by American capital while that resolution stood and the Febreristas remained in the Government."[19] The Colorados, on the other hand, were held in high regard by U.S. officials. The party's leaders, predominantly rural landowners, were generally considered to be "very friendly toward the U.S. and interested in U.S. assistance in building up Paraguay." Party leader Federico Chaves, who had privately assured United States officials in Asunción that the Colorados were dedicated to freedom of speech and free elections in Paraguay, was described by the State Department as "staunch[ly] democratic in ideals and actuation." Chaves's major rival for leadership of the party, Juan Natalicio González, also was viewed with favor by the State Department for having "praised the Good Neighbor Policy" and for having declared that he was "amazed that a country as strong as the U.S. could be so patient, so considerate, and so just in its relations with its weak neighbors." Natalicio González, the State Department noted with pleasure, was also on record as stating that "the great effort the Government of the U.S. was making to treat all nations, regardless of size and power, on a basis of perfect equality and of respect for sovereignty and independence of all peoples, was so important to the peace of the world and to the welfare of small nations in particular, that every country should do all it could to reciprocate this attitude in order to insure that the policy should be successful and lasting."[20]

Upon entering the coalition government, the Colorados soon justified Washington's assessment of them. In September 1946, seven weeks after Natalicio González and Chaves had been named to Morínigo's cabinet as ministers of finance and public works respectively, Paraguay concluded a reciprocal trade agreement with the United States—after Morínigo had previously resisted persistent United States efforts to negotiate such an agreement for nearly six years. By the terms of the 1946 trade treaty, Paraguay granted tariff concessions to United States iron and steel products, electrical equipment, automotive products, tractors, refrigerators, radios, telephones, and office equipment, while the United States pledged reciprocal concessions for Paraguayan quebracho, *yerba maté*, petit-grain oil, and *urunday* extract.[21]

After ousting their Febrerista rivals in January 1947, the Colorados continued to impress United States observers by issuing a steady stream of public pronouncements calculated to win favor in Washington. A new national party platform was immediately promulgated, which dedicated the Colorados to "democratic government and closer inter-American cooperation." Meanwhile, the official Colorado newspaper was announcing that "the Colorado Party does not believe in the theory of the 'absorbing State' or in the unnatural thesis that all foreign capital is 'imperialist' capital which should be combatted." "The role of the State as a regulatory body should be kept within proper limits," party leader Chaves told the nation. Paraguay's most pressing problem, he added, was to "attract capital."[22] "The new government should be a vast improvement over the preceding one," Beaulac informed the State Department in mid January. "The Colorado Party . . . looks toward the United States, and the new government has lost no time in making that clear. I recommend that the Government of the United States reciprocate this cooperative attitude in every reasonable and practicable manner."[23]

Despite their democratic rhetoric, however, the Colorados were simultaneously moving to entrench themselves permanently in power by means of the time-honored tactics of repression endogenous to the Paraguayan political system. Denied the spoils of office for some 43 years, the Colorados had no intention of surrendering power or sharing it with their competitors. Indeed, after ousting the Febreristas, the Colorados immediately imposed a new "temporary" ban on "political meetings and manifestations hostile to persons or institutions in Asunción." Within two weeks, all opposition newspapers had been confiscated, and Febrerista, Liberal, and Communist leaders had fled into exile or hiding. By February, Paraguay's court system and civil service had been exclusively turned over to Colorado-party functionaries, the key military and police commands had been filled by Colorado officers, and the national military academy had again begun to admit as officer-candidates only students from carefully screened Colorado family backgrounds.[24]

As the Colorados cemented their hold on the government, Paraguay's opposition parties joined together in a desperate last-ditch effort to prevent the consolidation of a new Colorado hegemony. In as unlikely a "marriage of convenience" as Paraguayan politics had ever produced, the Febreristas, the Communists, and the Liberals merged their forces and in March 1947 launched an insurrection against the Asunción government, seizing the important military garrison at Concepción, 130 miles north of the capital, and from there, rapidly bringing the entire northern half of the country under their control. Almost immediately, a majority of the army, navy, and air force deserted to the rebel forces, alienated by the new regime's "Coloradoization" of the Paraguayan armed forces. Badly outnumbered, the Colorados mobilized their barefoot rural peasant followers—their *py nandí*, or "shoeless ones" in Paraguay's native Guaraní language—and prepared to defend with force the party's long-awaited return to power.[25] Soon, full-scale civil war had broken out. As the fighting escalated, a bemused Morínigo chided United

"United They Will Save Democracy," Colorado-party poster issued during 1947 civil war, featuring (*left to right*) a Colorado *py nandi* peasant "volunteer" and a Paraguayan Army soldier (the original is attached to despatch no. 2715, True-blood to Marshall, 21 June 1947, DS834.00/6-2147, National Archives, Washington, D.C.).

109

States officials over the results of democratization in Paraguay. During the six years that he had governed the country without the assistance of a political party, "there had been no trouble," he reminded the U.S. chargé in Asunción; "it was only since the political parties came into the picture and civil liberties [were] restored that there had been difficulties." The course of events, Morínigo added sardonically, seemed "ironical indeed."[26]

The five-months' civil war of 1947 was bitter and destructive, with both sides shooting prisoners and burning enemy property. After some four months of desultory skirmishing and general stalemate along the northern front, rebel forces suddenly swept around the main Colorado army and moved southward against weakly-defended Asunción, leaving the Colorados' forces outflanked in the north and racing to catch up. As they descended upon the capital in early August, the rebels announced over their radio that the Colorado-party president's "filthy corpse" and those of Higinio Morínigo, Natalicio González, and other government officials would soon "hang from a rope." Against the rebel assault, Asunción's desperately outmanned Colorados deployed the last of their barefoot peasant reserves and an artillery regiment under the command of Alfredo Stroessner, a fast-rising young army officer who had remained loyal to the Colorados during the fighting. At the last moment, as rebel units penetrated to within one thousand yards of Morínigo's residence, the government's main peasant forces finally reached the capital after a desperate thirteen-day forced march from the north. Throwing themselves into the battle, they broke the assault and scattered the rebel forces, effectively bringing the civil war to a close.[27]

A week later, at the 1947 Inter-American Conference for the Maintenance of Continental Peace and Security in Rio de Janeiro, new Paraguayan Foreign Minister Federico Chaves informed United States Secretary of State George Marshall that the Colorados were "a democratic party" and "a close friend and supporter of the United States." Expressing his hope that Washington would "continue to help" Paraguay "in the fields of public health, economy, and military training," Chaves assured Marshall that "should hostilities occur between the 'totalitarian East' and 'democratic West' . . . , Paraguay would unreservedly stand by the U.S."[28] Meanwhile, back in Paraguay, the Colorado victory in the civil war had given way to an interlude of "Colorado terror," as the demobilized *py nandi* troops were permitted to engage in a spree of looting, rape, torture, and murder against rebel partisans that eventually forced an estimated four hundred thousand persons—including most of Paraguay's labor leaders and skilled workers—to flee into exile.[29] In February 1948, Natalicio González replaced Morínigo as president, in a one-candidate election so rigidly controlled that even write-in votes were prohibited.[30] The Colorados were now in full control of the Paraguayan government. They remain in power to the present day.

Conclusion

United States power and influence in southeastern South America expanded tremendously during the twelve years of Franklin D. Roosevelt's presidency. Between 1933 and the end of World War II, the United States overcame British and German commercial competition and emerged as the region's dominant industrial trading partner (see graph 1). Total United States trade and industrial export sales in the region increased by 496 and 711 percent respectively during the period.[1] The expanding presence was particularly striking in Paraguay, a remote and relatively inaccessible hemispheric backwater far removed from the United States orbit prior to 1933. During the Roosevelt years, Paraguay's trade with the United States increased by 1,364 percent, while Paraguayan purchases of United States industrial products rose by 1,594 percent.[2] Equally observable was the growth in the sheer numbers of United States citizens in Paraguay. As late as 1939, Paraguay's entire American colony numbered no more than thirty. Four years later, that figure had swelled to over two hundred, as a steady stream of diplomats; military officers; agricultural, public-health, and fiscal experts; highway and airport engineers; businessmen; teachers; nurses; and exchange students poured into the country. By 1943, the staff of the United States embassy in Asunción had been enlarged so conspicuously that the U.S. ambassador was warning the State Department of the danger of negative "psychological repercussions" on the part of the Paraguayans if the number of official United States representatives expanded further.[3]

To evaluate the Roosevelt administration's Latin American policy in quantitative terms of United States expansionism is not necessarily to indict its architects and practitioners as malevolent imperialists. As heirs to Woodrow Wilson's "liberal internationalist" world vision, Roosevelt, Hull, and Welles undoubtedly believed that a United States–led

113

liberal world order of capitalist democracies, linked interdependently through mutually profitable free trade, was the surest path to international peace and prosperity. Likewise, they were undoubtedly sincere in their conviction that the ethnocentrically conceived private-enterprise/ foreign-investment development model which they and their overseas representatives urged other nations to adopt was the most efficacious economic-development formula available. From this perspective, the

GRAPH 1

UNITED STATES, BRITISH, GERMAN TRADE
WITH SOUTHEASTERN SOUTH AMERICA, 1933–46.

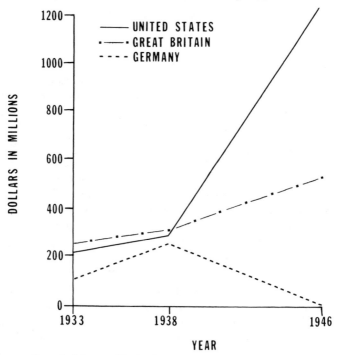

Compiled from table 1, chapter 3, and table 6, chapter 7.

expansion of United States power and influence in the Western Hemisphere during the period of Roosevelt's presidency could be interpreted as both an altruistic and a pragmatic campaign to construct a prosperous, stable new hemispheric order mutually beneficial to the United States *and* the nations of Latin America.

Nevertheless, measured by its record in southeastern South America, Roosevelt's Latin American policy revealed itself less as an example of "liberal internationalism" than of "liberal imperialism"—a concerted drive to achieve informal United States hegemony in a far-distant region of the hemisphere.[4] Although its focus and tactics passed through several distinct phases between 1933 and 1945, the "Good Neighbor policy" as applied to southeastern South America was consistently motivated by considerations of national economic self-interest. Initially designed to open new export markets in the region for United States industrial goods, as the New Dealers struggled desperately to overcome a debilitating domestic depression, the policy was later transformed into a weapon to combat the expansionist influence of a rival Northern Hemisphere industrial power, as Germany challenged the United States for primacy in the region. By its final phase, it had become an instrument to reorient southeastern South America's political economy in a direction conducive to further United States economic penetration. The central unifying thread that linked these successive phases together was the Roosevelt administration's active promotion of United States trade and investment in the region. Indeed, if any major element of the Good Neighbor policy represented a significant departure from established patterns of United States expansion and intervention in the hemisphere, it was the Roosevelt administration's innovative use of foreign aid as an instrument to advance traditional U.S. hegemonic aspirations.

The administration's use of foreign aid as a device to expand the United States' sphere of influence in Latin America was exemplified by the course of United States–Paraguayan relations during the pivotal years from 1939 to 1943. At each critical juncture in its relations with the Estigarribia and Morínigo regimes during this period, the Roosevelt administration consistently relied on material inducements to draw Paraguay into an expanding United States orbit and away from that of Nazi Germany. Export-Import Bank credits of $3.5 million prompted Estigarribia to align Paraguay firmly at the side of the United States in June 1939. An offer of $11 million in lend-lease military aid in April 1941 and subsequent United States hints of several additional millions of dollars in economic-development assistance were instrumental in influencing the Morínigo regime's decision, at the January 1942 Rio Conference, to accept United States hemispheric leadership during World War II. Export-Import Bank credits of $3 million kept Paraguay from defecting from the United States orbit in May 1942. Considered separately, these United States initiatives appear to have been motivated primarily by short-range "political factors" or "security factors"—the desire to assist the machinations of a favored ally (Estigarribia) in Paraguayan domestic politics during 1939; the need to elicit the Morínigo regime's acceptance of United States leadership against a potential Axis military threat to the hemisphere after Pearl Harbor; the desire to protect the only remotely "pro-Allied" political faction in the Paraguayan government (the Tiempistas) from ouster by pro-Axis military elements in 1942. From a macrolevel perspective, however, it is impossible to isolate individual United States aid initiatives in Paraguay from the broader context of a global power struggle between the United States and Germany, a consummate power struggle between rival industrial nations, in which economic factors (export markets, foreign investments, access to natural resources, etc.) were scarcely peripheral. It was no mere coincidence that each United States aid grant consistently drew Paraguay into a closer economic "partnership" with the United States, a partnership that ultimately served the interests of United States manufacturers, exporters, highway-construction companies, oil companies, airlines, telecommunications firms, and so forth, as those entities competed internationally against economic rivals based in Germany and other European industrial nations.

To suggest that the Roosevelt administration's Latin American policy had as its underlying *motive* the material self-interest of the United States is not, of course, to pass normative judgment upon that policy, but simply to recognize a fundamental truism of international relations: that nations act in their own self-interest, defined largely in economic terms of prosperity, productivity, and power. Measured by their *impact* on the political and economic structures of Paraguay, however, the Roosevelt administration's policies can be judged to have had far-reaching negative consequences. In its relations with the Estigarribia and Morínigo regimes between 1939 and 1943, the administration had employed foreign aid to "purchase" nominal Paraguayan alignment with the United States in the latter's power struggle against Germany. After mid 1944, foreign aid increasingly became a lever to structure postwar Paraguayan politics into a pattern more favorable to United States interests. The results, from the Paraguayan perspective, were less than edifying: a bitter and destructive civil war, the elimination of an honest and nationalistic dictatorship committed to at least a limited program of progressive reforms, and its replacement by a political party representing the corrupt "old order" of pre-1940 Paraguayan politics. In the economic sphere, United States foreign aid was largely concentrated in rural highway construction and agricultural-modernization programs, while the Roosevelt administration simultaneously withheld assistance for the industrial-development and hydroelectric-power projects through which the Morínigo regime hoped to structurally transform Paraguay's backward economy and achieve a modicum of economic self-sufficiency. Rather than contributing to balanced economic development, United States aid served to reinforce the traditional agricultural base of Paraguay's economy, in effect perpetuating Paraguayan underdevelopment and economic dependence.

Nevertheless, to focus on the motives and consequences of *United States* initiatives is not to characterize inter-American relations during the World War II era as a simple process of unilateral "penetration" of innocent Latin American "victims" by an imperialistic "Colossus of the North." The record of United States–Latin American wartime relations suggests, in fact, that factors of national economic self-interest shaped the actions of *both* sides in the inter-American equation and that, if anything, a constant two-way flow of *"mutual opportunism"* and *"reciprocal exploitation"* lay at the core of the hemispheric relationship. For if United States policies toward southeastern South America were consistently based on considerations of material self-interest, it is equally apparent that governmental leaders throughout southeastern South America formulated *their* foreign policies primarily on the basis of the economic opportunities and risks presented by the unstable and competitive international environment of the wartime era. To assert, for example, that the Roosevelt administration "purchased" Paraguayan alignment in the United States orbit between 1939 and 1943 is at the same time to state that successive Paraguayan administrations—"liberals" and "authoritarian nationalists" alike—deliberately and willfully "sold" their nation's international alignment in exchange for payments in the form of United States financial, technical, and military assistance. The primacy of material considerations in the process of Latin American foreign-policy formulation has perhaps never been more graphically illustrated than at the January 1942 Rio Conference, where each southeastern South American nation carefully calculated the long-range cost-benefits of a decision to align with the United States against Germany.

Ultimately, of course, the "transaction" proved to be an unequal one. Receipt of foreign aid constituted a virtual end in itself for Latin American leaders, whereas for United States officials the dispensing of that aid was merely a means through which to achieve broader economic ends. Wartime alignment with the United States produced material rewards—particularly in the form of Export-Import Bank development credits—for cooperative Latin American governments, but United States aid inevitably brought in its wake increased sales of U.S. equipment; an influx of U.S. engineers, technicians, and advisers; and new forms of United States leverage over the subsequent policy options of the recipient governments. As Higinio Morínigo discovered at the end of World War II, acceptance of United States assistance could dangerously increase the recipient's susceptibility to United States manipulative pressures. Nevertheless, from the perspective of Paraguayan (and Brazilian) wartime leaders, an unprecedented bonanza of United States aid was viewed as satisfactory compensation for an increased degree of subordination to United States leadership in international affairs.

The same material factors of aid, trade, and investment which shaped the pattern of United States–Latin American relations during the World War II era continued to define the basic nature of inter-American tactical interactions in the ensuing postwar decades. Roosevelt's successors in the White House consistently adopted his "good neighbor" approach as a prototype for their own policy initiatives toward Latin America, utilizing ever-increasing quantities of ostensibly altruistic United States foreign aid to purchase international support, reward clientelism, discourage nationalism, and generally promote the open, interdependent, liberal world order which remained synonymous with United States economic prosperity and material well-being. Concomitantly, a majority of postwar Latin American leaders continued, in their foreign-policy formulations, to apply the fundamental lesson of the World War II era: that alignment with the United States in world affairs was an effective and reliable path to material bounty. Through the first three postwar decades, for example, successive Colorado governments continued to align Paraguay firmly within the United States orbit. In return, they received some $200.1 million in United States foreign aid between 1946 and 1975.[5] Meanwhile, direct United States private investments in Paraguay were simultaneously rising from $9 million[6] to $53 million.[7] By 1975, the total volume of United States trade and industrial export sales in Paraguay had reached $51.9 million and $32.6 million respectively (increases of 841 percent and 626 percent, respectively, over 1946 levels),[8] while the total number of United States citizens in Paraguay had grown to more than twelve hundred.[9] More than three decades after World War II, the United States and Paraguay remained locked in a mutually exploitative and inherently unequal "partnership" that seemed destined to survive until a further evolutionary change in international great-power hierarchies brought about a new configuration in international alignments.

Notes

AS   Records of the Army Staff

DGFP   United States, Department of State, *Documents on German Foreign Policy, 1918–1945*

DS   General Records of the Department of State

FEA   Records of the Foreign Economic Administration

FRUS   United States, Department of State, *Foreign Relations of the United States*

OIAA   General Records of the Office of Inter-American Affairs

OSS   Records of the Office of Strategic Services

RG   Record Group

WD   Records of the War Department General and Special Staffs

Chapter 1

1. Arthur M. Schlesinger, Jr., *The Crisis of the Old Order, 1919–33* (Boston: Houghton Mifflin Co., 1957), chap. 1; William E. Leuchtenburg, *The Perils of Prosperity, 1914–32* (Chicago: University of Chicago Press, 1958), chap. 13; David A. Shannon, *Between the Wars: America, 1919–1941* (Boston: Houghton Mifflin Co., 1965), chap. 5.

2. Franklin D. Roosevelt, *The Public Papers and Addresses of Franklin D. Roosevelt,* comp. Samuel I. Rosenman, 13 vols. (New York: Random House, 1938–50), 2:11–15.

3. Quoted in William E. Leuchtenburg, *Franklin D. Roosevelt and the New Deal, 1932–1940* (New York: Harper & Row, 1963), p. 336.

4. Ibid., pp. 41–94; James MacGregor Burns, *Roosevelt: The Lion and the Fox* (New York: Harcourt, Brace & World, Inc., 1956), pp. 242–43, 322; Shannon, *Between the Wars,* pp. 153–60, 182.

5. Quoted in Carl N. Degler, *Out of Our Past: The Forces That Shaped Modern America,* rev. ed. (New York and Evanston: Harper & Row, 1970), p. 408.

6. Leuchtenburg, *Perils of Prosperity,* p. 248.
7. Shannon, *Between the Wars,* pp. 169–70. For background, see Lloyd C. Gardner, *Economic Aspects of New Deal Diplomacy* (Madison: University of Wisconsin Press, 1964), chaps. 1 and 2; Dick Steward, *Trade and Hemisphere: The Good Neighbor Policy and Reciprocal Trade* (Columbia: University of Missouri Press, 1975), chap. 1.
8. John A. Garraty, "The New Deal, National Socialism, and the Great Depression," *American Historical Review* 78 (October 1973): 908.
9. Frederick L. Schuman, *The Nazi Dictatorship: A Study in Social Pathology and the Politics of Fascism,* 2d ed., rev. (New York: Alfred A. Knopf, 1939), pp. 104, 402.
10. Eugen J. Weber, *Varieties of Fascism: Doctrines of Revolution in the Twentieth Century* (Princeton, N.J.: Van Nostrand Co., Inc., 1964), p. 79.
11. Ibid., chaps. 1–4, 6, 14; Harry Roderick Kedward, *Fascism in Western Europe, 1900–45* (New York: New York University Press, 1971), pp. 30–32.
12. Weber, *Varieties of Fascism,* pp. 13–19, 23–25, 32, 139; Kedward, *Fascism in Western Europe,* pp. 29–31; Francis L. Carsten, *The Rise of Fascism* (Berkeley and Los Angeles: University of California Press, 1967), pp. 230–36.
13. A. James Gregor, *The Ideology of Fascism: The Rationale of Totalitarianism* (New York: Free Press, 1969), pp. xii–xiii, 332, 368, 380–81; Weber, *Varieties of Fascism,* pp. 26–28, 32–34, 47–48, 53, 62, 74–81; Carsten, *Rise of Fascism,* pp. 230–32.
14. Among the movements were the English Guild Socialists, Charles Maurras's Action française, Heinrich Pesch's German Social Catholicism, and the Vatican doctrines of Popes Leo XIII and Pius XI.
15. Ralph H. Bowen, *German Theories of the Corporative State, with Special Reference to the Period 1870–1919* (New York: Whittlesey House, 1947), pp. 1–2, 5–6, 13–22, 75–79, 116–17; Philippe C. Schmitter, "Still the Century of Corporatism?" in *The New Corporatism: Socio-Political Structures in the Iberian World,* ed. Fredrick B. Pike and Thomas Stritch (Notre Dame, Ind.: University of Notre Dame Press, 1974), pp. 85–88, 93–94, 102–5, 115–25. Several historians have detected a degree of corporatist functional representation in Franklin D. Roosevelt's National Recovery Administration, with its self-governing codes for business and labor groups. See, for example, Garraty, "The New Deal," pp. 912–15, and Burns, *Roosevelt,* p. 198.
16. Weber, *Varieties of Fascism,* p. 36; Carsten, *Rise of Fascism,* p. 232; Gregor, *Ideology of Fascism,* pp. xii–xiii; S. J. Woolf, "Did a Fascist Economic System Exist?" in *The Nature of Fascism,* ed. S. J. Woolf (New York: Random House, 1968), pp. 128, 135, 143. As Sir Oswald Mosley, leader of the British Union of Fascists, explained, "Capitalism is the system by which capital uses the Nation for its own purposes. Fascism is the system by which the Nation uses capital for its own purposes. Private enterprise is permitted and encouraged so long as it coincides with the national interests. Private enterprise is not permitted when it conflicts with the national interests.

Under Fascism private enterprise may serve but not exploit. This is secured by the Corporative System which lays down the limits within which industry may operate and those limits are the welfare of the Nation." Quoted in Kedward, *Fascism in Western Europe*, p. 216.

17. Woolf, "Did a Fascist Economic System Exist?" pp. 138–39, 143.
18. Weber, *Varieties of Fascism*, pp. 52–53, 55–57, 61; Carsten, *Rise of Fascism*, pp. 232–34; George L. Mosse, "The Genesis of Fascism," in *International Fascism, 1920–1945*, ed. Walter Laqueur and George L. Mosse (New York: Harper & Row, Publishers, Inc., 1966), p. 14.
19. Weber, *Varieties of Fascism*, pp. 26–28, 60, 71–74; Kedward, *Fascism in Western Europe*, p. 214.
20. Quoted in Weber, *Varieties of Fascism*, p. 86.
21. Ibid., pp. 83–87; Garraty, "The New Deal," pp. 909–10, 915, 918, 944; Woolf, "Did a Fascist Economic System Exist?" pp. 132, 138.

CHAPTER 2

1. Stanley J. Stein and Barbara H. Stein, *The Colonial Heritage of Latin America: Essays on Economic Dependence in Perspective* (New York: Oxford University Press, 1970), chap. 6.
2. Ibid., chap. 5; J. Fred Rippy, *British Investments in Latin America, 1822–1949: A Case Study of the Operations of Private Enterprise in Retarded Regions* (Minneapolis: University of Minnesota Press, 1959); Desmond Christopher St. Martin Platt, *Latin America and British Trade, 1806–1914* (London: Adam & Charles Black Ltd., 1972); D. C. M. Platt, ed., *Business Imperialism, 1840–1930: An Inquiry Based on British Experience in Latin America* (Oxford, England: Clarendon Press, 1977). Also see Henry Stanley Ferns, *Britain and Argentina in the Nineteenth Century* (Oxford, England: Clarendon Press, 1960), and Richard Graham, *Britain and the Onset of Modernization in Brazil, 1850–1914* (London: Cambridge University Press, 1968).
3. Stein and Stein, *Colonial Heritage of Latin America*, chaps. 5 and 6; Charles W. Anderson, *Politics and Economic Change in Latin America* (Princeton, N.J.: Van Nostrand Co., Inc., 1967), chap. 1.
4. Sanford A. Mosk, "Latin America and the World Economy, 1850–1914," *Inter-American Economic Affairs* 2 (Winter 1948): 53–82; William P. Glade, *The Latin American Economies: A Study of Their Institutional Evolution* (New York: American Book, Van Nostrand Reinhold, 1969), pp. 347–401; and Celso Furtado, *The Economic Growth of Brazil: A Survey from Colonial to Modern Times*, translated by Ricardo W. de Aguiar and Eric Charles Drysdale (Berkeley: University of California Press, 1963), chaps. 30 and 31.
5. The following account of sociopolitical trends in the Iberic world during the interwar period is drawn from Stanley G. Payne, *A History of Spain and Portugal*, 2 vols. (Madison: University of Wisconsin Press, 1973); Marvin Goldwert, *Democracy, Militarism, and Nationalism in Argentina,*

1930–1966: An Interpretation (Austin: University of Texas Press, for the Institute of Latin American Studies, 1972); Robert A. Potash, *The Army and Politics in Argentina,* vol. 1: *1928–1945* (Stanford, Calif.: Stanford University Press, 1969); Thomas E. Skidmore, *Politics in Brazil, 1930–1964: An Experiment in Democracy* (New York: Oxford University Press, 1967); John D. Wirth, *The Politics of Brazilian Development, 1930–1954* (Stanford, Calif.: Stanford University Press, 1970); Robert M. Levine, *The Vargas Regime: The Critical Years, 1934–1938* (New York and London: Columbia University Press, 1970); and Howard J. Wiarda, "Corporatism and Development in the Iberic-Latin World: Persistent Strains and New Variations," in *New Corporatism,* ed. Pike and Stritch, pp. 3–33. Also see: James M. Malloy, ed., *Authoritarianism and Corporatism in Latin America* (Pittsburgh, Pa.: University of Pittsburgh Press, 1977), especially Malloy's introductory essay, "Authoritarianism and Corporatism in Latin America: The Modal Pattern," pp. 3–19. Also useful for Argentina is *Prologue to Perón: Argentina in Depression and War, 1930–1943,* ed. Mark Falcoff and Ronald H. Dolkart (Berkeley: University of California Press, 1975), chaps. 1, 2, 3, and 5; Marysa Gerassi, "Argentine Nationalism of the Right: The History of an Ideological Development, 1930–1946" (Ph.D. diss., Columbia University, 1964).

6. For a fuller discussion of the "role expansion" of the Latin American armed forces after World War I, see Robert A. Potash's "The Twentieth-Century Argentine Military," Frank D. McCann, Jr.'s "The Twentieth-Century Brazilian Military," and Frederick M. Nunn's "The Twentieth-Century Chilean Military," papers presented at the ninetieth annual convention of the American Historical Association, Atlanta, Georgia, 28 December 1975.

7. See, for example, Margaret Todaro Williams, "Integralism and the Brazilian Catholic Church," *Hispanic American Historical Review* 54 (August 1974): 431–52; and John J. Kennedy, *Catholicism, Nationalism, and Democracy in Argentina* (Notre Dame, Ind.: University of Notre Dame Press, 1958), pp. 139–45, 180–83. Not coincidentally, the first Catholic Action movements and Social Catholic political parties in Latin America appeared in the aftermath of World War I.

8. Goldwert, *Democracy, Militarism, and Nationalism in Argentina,* chap. 1; Gerassi, "Argentine Nationalism of the Right," chap. 2.

9. See particularly Skidmore, *Politics in Brazil,* chap. 1; Levine, *Vargas Regime,* introduction and chaps. 1 and 2; Potash, *Army and Politics in Argentina,* chaps. 1–7; and Goldwert, *Democracy, Militarism, and Nationalism in Argentina,* introduction and chaps. 1–4. For Paraguay, see below, chap. 4. Although no purely authoritarian nationalist faction came to power in Uruguay, during 1933/34, incumbent president Gabriel Terra carried out an internal coup d'état, dissolved the Uruguayan legislature, and established a short-lived dictatorship. In addition, a militant authoritarian sector, which was led by Luís Alberto Herrera and Eduardo Víctor

Haedo and supported by army and church elements, was a vocal factor in Uruguayan politics throughout the 1930s and 1940s.

10. Potash, *Army and Politics in Argentina,* chap. 3.

11. José Luís Romero, *A History of Argentine Political Thought* (Stanford, Calif.: Stanford University Press, 1963), chap. 9.

12. Skidmore, *Politics in Brazil,* chap. 1; Levine, *Vargas Regime,* chaps. 5–7; E. Bradford Burns, *A History of Brazil* (New York: Columbia University Press, 1970), chap. 6.

13. Potash, *Army and Politics in Argentina,* chap. 3.

14. Levine, *Vargas Regime,* chap. 7; Kenneth Paul Erickson, *The Brazilian Corporative State and Working-Class Politics* (Berkeley: University of California Press, 1977), chaps. 2 and 3.

15. Wiarda, "Corporatism and Development in the Iberic-Latin World," p. 3; Woolf, "Did a Fascist Economic System Exist?" p. 149; Office of Strategic Services research and analysis report no. 2965: "New Trends Toward Totalitarianism in Argentina," 10 March 1945, Lot Files, General Records of the Department of State, RG 59, United States National Archives, Washington, D.C. (hereinafter cited as DS). In Uruguay, during the Terra dictatorship of 1933–34, several corporative revisions of the Uruguayan constitution were formulated but never implemented. See Martin Weinstein, *Uruguay: The Politics of Failure* (Westport, Conn.: Greenwood Press, 1975), pp. 70–76. It should also be noted that Mexico's monolithic state party, the Partido revolucionario institucional, or PRI, which was organized during the 1920s and 1930s, was, with its various military, peasant, trade-union, business, professional, and bureaucratic representational sectors, essentially corporatist in nature.

16. Goldwert, *Democracy, Militarism, and Nationalism in Argentina,* chap. 2.

17. Levine, *Vargas Regime,* chaps. 7 and 8; Erickson, *Brazilian Corporative State,* chaps. 2 and 3.

18. Quoted in George I. Blanksten, *Perón's Argentina* (Chicago: University of Chicago Press, 1953), pp. 258–59. According to a recent analysis by a British political scientist, Perón's governmental program "was not designed to radically transform the national economic and social structure, but it is ironic that its conservative tendencies were lost upon the conservative critics of the regime, who saw only the illiberalism which accompanied it. The Peronists were overthrown by those who objected to their apparent radicalism and who did not understand how truly conservative their vision of society was. The novelty to which they objected lay in the fact that while Peronism required the support of the common people, the mediatory role normally performed on their behalf by the political parties was now to be performed by the State. Thus the Peronists sought a revolution in political culture without any serious changes in structure, and this contradiction accounts for their failure to transcend personalism and create an effective party" (Walter Little, "Party and State in Peronist Argentina,

1945–1955," *Hispanic American Historical Review* 53 [November 1973]: 661).

19. Wirth, *Politics of Brazilian Development;* Furtado, *Economic Growth of Brazil,* chaps. 31–33; Goldwert, *Democracy, Militarism, and Nationalism in Argentina,* chaps. 2, 4, and 5; Blanksten, *Perón's Argentina,* chap. 10; Robert J. Alexander, *The Perón Era* (New York: Columbia University Press, 1951), pp. 154–69.

CHAPTER 3

1. The descending geographic scale of United States economic influence in Latin America can be seen in the following table, which lists the United States' share of the foreign trade of Latin America in 1938:

	IMPORTS FROM THE UNITED STATES (% of total imports)	EXPORTS TO THE UNITED STATES (% of total exports)
Cuba	71	76
Mexico	58	67
Central America	52	67
Venezuela	56	13
Colombia	51	53
Ecuador	35	37
Brazil	24	34
Peru	34	26
Chile	28	15
Bolivia	25	5
Paraguay	10	12
Argentina	18	9
Uruguay	12	4

The low export figures for Venezuela and Bolivia are misleading, because Venezuela's leading export—oil—was first exported to the Dutch West Indies for refining, and Bolivia's dominant export—tin—was first shipped to England for smelting, before either reached its ultimate destination, the United States. Source: Richard F. Behrendt, *Inter-American Economic Relations: Problems and Prospects* (New York: Committee on International Economic Policy, 1948), p. 11.

2. United States, Department of State, *Report of the Delegates of the United States of America to the Seventh International Conference of American States, Montevideo, Uruguay, December 3–26, 1933* (Washington, D.C.: Government Printing Office, 1934), pp. 18–19, 196–98; Gardner, *Economic Aspects of New Deal Diplomacy,* p. 58.

3. Behrendt, *Inter-American Economic Relations,* pp. 7–8.

4. Edwin Lieuwen, *U.S. Policy in Latin America: A Short History* (New York: Frederick A. Praeger, Inc., for the Council on Foreign Relations, 1965), pp. 69–70; David Green, *The Containment of Latin America: A History of the Myths and Realities of the Good Neighbor Policy* (Chicago: Quadrangle Books, 1971), pp. 21–22; Wirth, *Politics of Brazilian Development,*

pp. 22–23; Frank D. McCann, Jr., *The Brazilian-American Alliance, 1937–1945* (Princeton, N.J.: Princeton University Press, 1973), pp. 149–50; Stanley E. Hilton, *Brazil and the Great Powers, 1930–1939: The Politics of Trade Rivalry* (Austin: University of Texas Press, 1975), chap. 3.

5. Alton Frye, *Nazi Germany and the American Hemisphere, 1933–1941* (New Haven, Conn., and London: Yale University Press, 1967), pp. 72–74; Wirth, *Politics of Brazilian Development*, pp. 20, 43; McCann, *Brazilian-American Alliance*, pp. 150–52, 157, 164. The German Foreign Office recognized that the region's industrialization would work "to the disadvantage of the German export market" but believed that such an eventuality lay "far in the future, quite aside from the fact that we will not in any case be able in the long run to prevent such industrialization." United States Department of State, *Documents on German Foreign Policy, 1918–1945* (hereinafter cited as *DGFP*), ser. D, vol. 11 (Washington, D.C.: Government Printing Office, 1960), p. 1177, memorandum, Wiehl, director, Economic Policy Department, German Foreign Office, 23 January 1941.

6. J. Fred Rippy, "German Investments in Latin America," *Journal of Business of the University of Chicago* 21 (April 1948): 71–72.

7. Woolf, "Did a Fascist Economic System Exist?" pp. 139–40, 143.

8. Cordell Hull, *The Memoirs of Cordell Hull*, 2 vols. (New York: Macmillan Co., 1948), 1:813–14, 820–22; Wirth, *Politics of Brazilian Development*, p. 65.

9. Hull, *Memoirs*, 1:496, 821; Edwin Lieuwen, *Arms and Politics in Latin America* (New York: Frederick A. Praeger, Inc., 1961), pp. 188–91; *DGFP*, ser. D, vol. 10, pp. 529–30, Wiehl to German Missions in Argentina, Chile, Bolivia, Uruguay, 23 August 1940.

10. Whether such fears were warranted remains a topic of controversy. One recent analysis points out that "no records of any kind have come to light of Nazi plans for an actual invasion of North or South America," adding that Hitler "was not even able to strike effectively at Britain. . . . He was fully aware that he lacked the means even to contemplate an invasion of the Western Hemisphere and that it would be many years before the equipment necessary for such an enterprise could be assembled. Meanwhile he would need a long interval of peace to consolidate his gains in Europe." Norman Rich, *Hitler's War Aims*, vol. 2: *The Establishment of the New Order* (New York: W. W. Norton & Co., Inc., 1974), pp. 416–17. Others, while conceding the lack of hard evidence, argue that Hitler did plan a military conquest of the Americas and that German technology would soon have produced aircraft and missiles that could have assured a successful invasion. See, for example, Frye, *Nazi Germany and the American Hemisphere*, pp. 183–88.

11. Hull, *Memoirs*, 1:820–21; telegram no. 844, Lord Lothian, Washington, to Foreign Office, 27 May 1940, A3285/109/51, Correspondence of the British Foreign Office, Public Record Office, London (hereinafter cited as British Foreign Office); minute, Balfour, 29 May 1940, A3285/109/51, British For-

eign Office; Stetson Conn and Byron Fairchild, *The Western Hemisphere: The Framework of Hemisphere Defense,* vol. 12, pt. 1, of *United States Army in World War II,* ed. Kent Roberts Greenfield (Washington, D.C.: Government Printing Office, 1960), pp. 32–33. The besieged British concluded that "it would be disastrous to our whole position—political, economic, and alimentary—in South America were a Fascist Nazi coup to seize the River Plate to be successful," but also believed that "a Nazi coup that failed would work in our favour by bringing nearer American intervention: indeed if only the coup could be traced to instigation from Germany it might come close to being an infringement of the Monroe doctrine." Minutes, 22 May 1940, A3285/109/51, British Foreign Office.

12. "Totalitarian Activity in the Other American Republics," 10 January 1941, chap. 7, pp. 3–7, folder 331, box 79, Cordell Hull Papers, Library of Congress, Washington, D.C. (hereinafter cited as Hull MSS).

13. Quoted in Hans Louis Trefousse, *Germany and American Neutrality, 1939–1941* (New York: Bookman Associates, 1951), p. 56.

14. "Totalitarian Activity in the Other American Republics," 10 January 1941, chap. 7, pp. 1–2, 7, folder 331, box 79, Hull MSS.

15. Hull, *Memoirs,* 1:495.

16. Research and analysis report no. 667: "An Estimate of the Situation in South Brazil," 27 August 1942, Records of the Office of Strategic Services, RG 226, United States National Archives, Washington, D.C. (hereinafter cited as OSS). According to this OSS report, persons of German, Italian, and Japanese descent in southern Brazil and neighboring countries numbered as follows:

	TOTAL POPULATION	GERMAN	ITALIAN	JAPANESE
Brazil				
Rio Grande do Sul	3,336,000	516,000	300,000	100
Santa Catarina	1,182,000	275,000	50,000	498
Paraná	1,243,000	126,000	100,000	6,241
Argentina				
Misiones	168,831	31,000	4,000	0
Corrientes	508,261	2,000	22,000	10
Paraguay	936,000	17,000	7,000	600

17. Frye, *Nazi Germany and the American Hemisphere,* pp. 65–69, 78, 103, 106; William Simonson, "Nazi Infiltration in South America, 1933–1945" (Ph.D. diss., Tufts University, 1964), chaps. 2–10.

18. Memorandum, King to Duggan, 24 September 1940, DS819.00N/35.

19. Ibid.; telegram no. 140, Millington-Drake (Montevideo) to Foreign Office, 26 May 1940, A3285/109/51, British Foreign Office. There are indications that Hitler's actual intention was to "recover" the German immigrants for later use in colonizing and administering European territories conquered by German military forces. Rich, *Hitler's War Aims,* 2:418.

20. See, for example, United States, Department of State, *Report of the Dele-*

gation of the United States of America to the Eighth International Confer-ence of American States, Lima, Peru, December 9–27, 1938 (Washington, D.C.: Government Printing Office, 1941), pp. 203–4; United States, Depart-ment of State, *Report of the Delegate of the United States of America to the Meeting of the Foreign Ministers of the American Republics Held at Panama, September 23–October 3, 1939* (Washington, D.C.: Government Printing Office, 1940), pp. 33–39, 73; United States, Department of State, *Second Meeting of the Ministers of Foreign Affairs of the American Re-publics, Habana, July 21–30, 1940, Report of the Secretary of State* (Wash-ington, D.C.: Government Printing Office, 1941), pp. 9, 25, 46–55, 80–84.

21. J. Manuel Espinosa, *Inter-American Beginnings of U.S. Cultural Diplomacy, 1936–1948* (Washington, D.C.: Department of State, 1976); Hull, *Memoirs,* 1:610.

22. *New York Times,* 28 October 1941, p. 4; William L. Langer and S. Everett Gleason, *The Undeclared War, 1940–1941* (New York: Harper, for Council on Foreign Relations, 1953), p. 595; Irwin F. Gellman, "The New Deal's Use of Nazism in Latin America," in *Perspectives in American Diplomacy: Essays on Europe, Latin America, China, and the Cold War,* ed. Jules Davids (New York: Arno Press, 1976), pp. 197–200.

23. Mark Skinner Watson, *Chief of Staff: Prewar Plans and Preparations,* vol. 4, pt. 1, of *United States Army in World War II,* ed. Kent Roberts Green-field (Washington, D.C.: Government Printing Office, 1950), pp. 89–91; Lieuwen, *Arms and Politics in Latin America,* pp. 188–92.

24. Gardner, *Economic Aspects of New Deal Diplomacy,* pp. 63, 112, 126–28.

25. Green, *Containment of Latin America,* pp. 61, 74–75.

26. *General Policy Statement of the Export-Import Bank of Washington* (Wash-ington, D.C.: Government Printing Office, 1945).

27. Memorandum, Bidwell, Office of Inter-American Affairs, 23 June 1942, folder: "Post-War Planning," Central Files, General Records of the Office of Inter-American Affairs, RG 229, United States National Archives, Wash-ington, D.C. (hereinafter cited as OIAA).

28. Green, *Containment of Latin America,* pp. 75–77; Gardner, *Economic Aspects of New Deal Diplomacy,* pp. 127–28, 195.

29. Research and analysis report no. 132: "An Analysis of the Elements of Insecurity in Argentina," 7 October 1941, OSS; research and analysis report no. 154: "Report on the Attitude of Brazil toward the Establishment of Naval and Air Bases by the United States on Brazilian Territory," 21 No-vember 1941, OSS.

30. Donald Dozer, *Are We Good Neighbors? Three Decades of Inter-American Relations, 1930–1960* (Gainesville: University of Florida Press, 1959), pp. 53–54.

31. Despatch no. 80, Frost to Hull, 2 July 1941, DS811.20234/5. For Brazilian perceptions of the international environment of the 1930s, see Hilton, *Brazil and the Great Powers,* pp. 5–15, 31–33. A similar expression of views

by a leading Argentine policy-maker in 1942 is quoted in Javier Villanueva, "Economic Development," in *Prologue to Perón,* p. 208 n.30.

32. Dozer, *Are We Good Neighbors?* p. 61.

33. Ibid., p. 53.

34. Glen Barclay, *Struggle for a Continent: The Diplomatic History of South America, 1917–1945* (New York: New York University Press, 1972), pp. 120–21.

35. Research and analysis report no. 154: "Report on the Attitude of Brazil toward the Establishment of Naval and Air Bases by the United States on Brazilian Territory," 21 November 1941, OSS.

36. Fredrick B. Pike, "Corporatism and Latin American–United States Relations," in *New Corporatism,* ed. Pike and Stritch, pp. 144–49.

37. McCann, *Brazilian-American Alliance,* pp. 69, 117, 149, 153, 177; Hilton, *Brazil and the Great Powers,* passim.

38. Wirth, *Politics of Brazilian Development,* pp. 112–16.

39. United States, Department of State, *Foreign Relations of the United States* (hereinafter cited as *FRUS*), 1940, vol. 5, p. 600, memorandum of conversation, 22 January 1940; *FRUS,* 1940, 5:608, telegram no. 339, Caffery to Hull, 8 July 1940; *FRUS,* 1940, 5:609–10, letter, Welles to Jones, 7 August 1940; *FRUS,* 1940, 5:611, telegram no. 315, Hull to Caffery, 24 September 1940. Although assistance in the development of a Brazilian steel industry was detrimental to United States steel exporters, the Roosevelt administration made certain that U.S. private enterprise profited from the Volta Redonda project by stipulating that the $20 million loan was "for the purchase in the United States of materials and equipment for the mill and for the hiring of engineering and professional talent," reserving for the Export-Import Bank "the privilege of concurring in the selection of managerial officers, engineers, contractors and materials," and requiring the mill "to employ officers and engineers experienced in the manufacture of steel in the United States until successful operation has been assured" (ibid.). Also see Hilton, *Brazil and the Great Powers,* pp. 178, 181, 217–19.

CHAPTER 4

1. The following account of Paraguayan history to 1870 is drawn primarily from Harris Gaylord Warren, *Paraguay: An Informal History* (Norman: University of Oklahoma Press, 1949), chaps. 10–13; Philip Raine, *Paraguay* (New Brunswick, N.J.: Scarecrow Press, 1956), chaps. 3 and 4; George Pendle, *Paraguay: A Riverside Nation,* 3d ed. (London: Oxford University Press, for Royal Institute of International Affairs, 1967), pp. 15–22; and Paul H. Lewis, *The Politics of Exile: Paraguay's Febrerista Party* (Chapel Hill: University of North Carolina Press, 1968), pp. 3–17.

2. John Hoyt Williams, "Paraguay's Nineteenth-Century *Estancias de la República,*" *Agricultural History* 47 (July 1973): 206–15.

3. Officially, the National Republican Association.

4. Lewis claims that out of a total of two million pounds sterling borrowed

from the British banking firm of Baring Brothers in 1871/72, only 840,000 £ ever reached the Paraguayan treasury.

5. A native Paraguayan tree of extreme hardness (*quebracho* means, literally, "axe-breaker"), prized as a durable building material and as a source of tannin extract, a tanning agent indispensable to the shoe and leather-goods industries.

6. Warren, *Paraguay*, chap. 16; Raine, *Paraguay*, chap. 5; Pendle, *Paraguay*, pp. 23–31; Lewis, *Politics of Exile*, pp. 17–36.

7. David H. Zook, Jr., *The Conduct of the Chaco War* (New York: Bookman Associates, 1960), p. 241.

8. Raine, *Paraguay*, p. 223; Harris Gaylord Warren, "Political Aspects of the Paraguayan Revolution, 1936–1940," *Hispanic American Historical Review* 30 (February 1950): 5–6; Warren, *Paraguay*, pp. 315–19; Juan Stefanich, *El Paraguay nuevo: Por la democracia y la libertad hacia un nuevo ideario americano* (Buenos Aires: Editorial Claridad, 1943), pp. 47–56; Efraím Cardozo, *Breve historia del Paraguay* (Buenos Aires: Editorial Universitaria de Buenos Aires, 1965), p. 152; Carlos Pastore, *El Paraguay y la tiranía de Morínigo* (Montevideo: Editorial Antequera, 1947), pp. 53–55; Carlos Alberto, *Itinerario político del Paraguay, 1936–1949* (Asunción: Editorial "El País," 1950), p. 4; Rodolfo Bellani Nazeri, *Morínigo, un hombre de América* (Santiago, Chile: Editorial "Revista de las Américas," 1946), pp. 25–27, 32–33.

9. Lewis, *Politics of Exile*, pp. 30–32. During the 1940s, the United States embassy in Asunción devoted considerable attention to the background and evolution of the Paraguayan armed forces' politicization. For valuable analyses, based on interviews with key participants in the events of the 1930s, see despatch no. 1974, Frost to Hull, 8 April 1944, DS834.00/1324; despatch no. 2134, Frost to Hull, 27 May 1944, DS834.00/1342; despatch no. 346, Beaulac to Stettinius, 13 December 1944, DS834.00/12-1344; and despatch no. 788, Beaulac to Stettinius, 18 May 1945, DS834.00/5-1845.

10. The Chaco War produced a similar reaction of political alienation and nationalistic indignation among Bolivian field forces. After the war, young revolutionary officers, disaffected by what they perceived as unpardonable mismanagement of the war effort by Bolivia's civilian governmental leaders, formed a National Socialist party, overthrew the incumbent government, and—under the successive leadership of colonels David Toro and Germán Busch—attempted, between 1936 and 1939, to construct a "new Bolivia." During the 1940s, direction of the "Bolivian nationalist revolution" fell to Victor Paz Estenssoro and his Nationalist Revolutionary Movement, which subsequently emerged as the predominant force in Bolivian politics during the 1950s.

11. Raine, *Paraguay*, chaps. 6 and 7; Lewis, *Politics of Exile*, pp. 36–37; despatch no. 1974, Frost to Hull, 8 April 1944, DS834.00/1324, and despatch no. 2134, Frost to Hull, 27 May 1944, DS834.00/1342.

12. Despatch no. 27, Nicholson to Hull, 17 February 1934, DS834.001-Ayala, Eusebio/18.

13. Efraím Cardozo, *Paraguay independiente* (Barcelona: Salvat Editores, S.A., 1949), pp. 371–72.

14. Bellani Nazeri, *Morínigo,* p. 46; Lewis, *Politics of Exile,* p. 38.

15. Ayala was eventually exiled to Argentina, where he spent his remaining years as a lawyer for the Mihanovich shipping firm.

16. Quoted in Lewis, *Politics of Exile,* pp. 39–45.

17. Ibid., pp. 48–59; Warren, *Paraguay,* pp. 319–23; Warren, "Political Aspects of the Paraguayan Revolution," pp. 12–14; Juan Stefanich, *Renovación y liberación: La obra del Gobierno de Febrero* (Buenos Aires: Editorial El Mundo Nuevo, 1946), passim; Stefanich, *El Paraguay nuevo,* pp. 58–72; Policarpo Artaza, *Ayala, Estigarribia y el Partido Liberal* (Buenos Aires: Editorial Ayacucho, 1946), pp. 68–172.

18. Lewis, *Politics of Exile,* pp. 51–55, 59–62; Warren, "Political Aspects of the Paraguayan Revolution," pp. 14–16; Alberto, *Itinerario político del Paraguay,* pp. 5–7; Artaza, *Ayala, Estigarribia y el Partido Liberal,* p. 163.

19. Raine, *Paraguay,* p. 249. The economic policy of the new Paiva government was revealed on 20 August 1937. "With regard to Fiscal Expenditures," Finance Minister Luis Frescura announced, "the strictest economy must be the inflexible rule. . . . Concerning Fiscal Revenues . . . no reform will be made in the present taxing system which would create more onerous and new taxes. Too many taxes smother production, depress commerce, and influence the normal consumption of the population. The Execution of the Budget is to be carried out . . . complying with the duty of good administration, that is to say, spending the least possible in carrying out foreseen and determined public services. In this respect, an unbalanced budget must be avoided by all possible means" (quoted in despatch no. 440, Howard to Hull, 26 August 1937, DS834.00 Revolutions/40).

20. The name pays homage to the February 1936 revolution. As an organized party in exile, the Febreristas aligned themselves ideologically with Víctor Raúl Haya de la Torre's Peruvian Aprista party, a populist movement that addressed its appeal to the interests of workers, peasants, intellectuals, and the middle classes. Lewis, *Politics of Exile,* chap. 3; Robert J. Alexander, "The Latin American Aprista Parties," *Political Quarterly* 20 (July–September 1949): 236–47.

21. Cardozo, *Paraguay independiente,* p. 389; Alberto, *Itinerario político del Paraguay,* p. 9; Pastore, *Paraguay y la tiranía de Morínigo,* pp. 21–22.

22. Despatch no. 597, Howard to Hull, 22 April 1938, DS834.00/930; despatch no. 639, Howard to Hull, 14 July 1938, DS834.00/937.

23. *El Pais* (Asunción), 19 February 1940.

24. The principal author of the Paraguayan constitution of 1940, Justo Pastor Benítez, had served as Paraguay's minister to Mussolini's Italy during 1929

and 1930. Alberto, *Itinerario político del Paraguay,* p. 4; Lewis, *Politics of Exile,* p. 68.

25. Alberto, *Itinerario político del Paraguay,* pp. 8–11; Pendle, *Paraguay,* pp. 34–37; Warren, *Paraguay,* pp. 324–30; Lewis, *Politics of Exile,* pp. 66–69.

26. Richard Bourne, *Political Leaders of Latin America* (New York: Alfred A. Knopf, 1970), pp. 101–2.

27. Despatch no. 1264, Howard to Hull, 30 August 1940, DS834.5011/11; despatch no. 799, Frost to Hull, 18 February 1943, DS811.20234/17; despatch no. 1971, Frost to Hull, 7 April 1944, DS740.34112A/73; "The Impact of the War on the Economy of Paraguay," American Hemisphere Division of the Office of Economic Warfare Analysis, Board of Economic Warfare, 22 August 1942, folder: "Paraguay—Economic Conditions," Reports and Despatches from United States Missions in Latin America, Records of the Pan American Branch of the Bureau of Areas, Records of the Foreign Economic Administration, RG 169, United States National Archives, Washington, D.C. (hereinafter cited as FEA). The leading German firms in Asunción were Staudt, Krauch, Ferreterías Universal y Alemana, Tubos, Mannes, Mann, Wiske, and the German Bank. *FRUS,* 1944, 7:1482, telegram no. 98, Frost to Hull, 16 February 1944.

28. One such agent, Gustav Fettinger, summarized his activities in a 1939 report to Nazi officials in Munich: "I founded from 1932–1936 the Colonies Vista Alegre, Carlos, Pfannl, Colonia Taquara, and Borchay, all of which are situated around the town of Villa Rica in eastern Paraguay. . . . I have been running the German Mission in Paraguay in the spirit of National Socialism for six full years. Naturally I myself was a colonist, cultivated the jungle, and together with my wife built up a nice fruit hacienda." Subsequently, Fettinger reported, "I decided to sell my hacienda in Vista Alegre and go ahead to Ecuador [to continue] practical colonial work for Germany, to mobilize the Indians, the Spaniards, the Portuguese, and the Catholic Church against the USA, and in time to control and kill all Jewish resistance in America." Fettinger to Honig, chief of staff to General Ritter von Epp, Reichsleiter of the Colonial Political Office of the National Socialist German Workers Party, Munich, enclosure to despatch no. 649, Office of the Political Adviser, Headquarters United States Forces in Austria, to Department of State, 28 December 1945, DS862.20234/12-2845.

29. Despatch no. 1389, Howard to Hull, 4 January 1941, DS834.00/1049; letter, Frost to Duggan, 7 June 1941, DS834.00/1079; despatch no. 80, Frost to Hull, 2 July 1941, DS811.20234/5; "List of most objectionable Germans in Paraguay," enclosure to despatch no. 1860, Frost to Hull, 1 March 1944, DS740.00115 European War 1939/8849; despatch no. 1900, Frost to Hull, 17 March 1944, DS740.34112A/57; FBI Report, Hoover to Berle, 12 April 1944, Army-Intelligence Project Decimal File No. 080: Paraguay, Records of the Office of the Assistant Chief of Staff, G-2 (Intelligence), Records of the Army Staff, RG 319, United States National Archives, Washington, D.C. (hereinafter cited as AS).

30. The three companies were the Asunción Port Concession Corporation, International Products Corporation, and Algodones, S.A. (a cotton-ginning subsidiary of the Anderson, Clayton Company).

31. "Memorandum on Financial and Economic Conditions in Paraguay and Ways and Means of Improving Them," Estigarribia to Export-Import Bank, enclosure to letter, Pierson to Briggs, 17 December 1938, DS834.51/260; despatch no. 757, Dillingham to Hull, 22 December 1938, DS834.00/956; despatch no. 819, Howard to Hull, 6 April 1939, DS834.00/975; memorandum of conversation, 20 April 1939, DS834.51/267; despatch no. 1007, Howard to Hull, 28 November 1939, DS834.01A/12.

32. Despatch no. 438, Howard to Hull, 20 August 1937, DS834.00 Revolutions/31; memorandum, Butler to Duggan, n.d., DS834.00/910.

33. Letter, Welles to Pierson, 28 November 1938, DS834.154/51A; memorandum, Luthringer to Livesey, 4 January 1939, DS834.51/259; memorandum, Collado to Briggs, Duggan, Feis, Welles, 26 April 1939, DS834.51/270; enclosure to despatch no. 1, Frost to Hull, 2 May 1941, DS834.51/339. A particularly "unfavorable aspect of the [highway] project," the State Department's adviser on international economic affairs pointed out, "is that . . . it would make possible a four-fold increase in the production of cotton. This can hardly be regarded as an advantage from the point of view of the interests of the United States." "It would appear more advisable, from the point of view of this Government at least," a colleague concurred, "to attempt to find other directions in which this Government could by means of financial assistance aid in the economic reconstruction of Paraguay" (memorandum, Collado to Briggs, Feis, Welles, 6 February 1939, DS834.51/260).

34. Despatch no. 800, Dillingham to Hull, 9 March 1939, DS834.00/970.

35. Telegram no. 14, Howard to Hull, 11 May 1939, DS824.6363 St 2/360; telegram no. 87, Tuck to Hull, 11 May 1939, DS824.6363 St 2/359; despatch no. 516, Caldwell to Hull, 12 May 1939, DS824.6363 St 2/364; *New York Times*, 8 June 1939, p. 13; Bryce Wood, *The Making of the Good Neighbor Policy* (New York: W. W. Norton & Co., 1967), p. 186.

36. Memorandum of conversation, 24 May 1939, DS834.6363/45; memorandum of conversation, 13 September 1939, DS834.6363/50; telegram no. 12, Welles to Howard, 15 April 1940, DS834.6363/54.

37. Telegram no. 8, Hull to American Legation, Asunción, 14 June 1939, DS834.51/275; despatch no. 1007, Howard to Hull, 28 November 1939, DS834.01A/12.

38. *El País* (Asunción), 1 June 1939.

39. Memorandum, Hooker, 4 October 1940, DS834.51/321; "The Impact of the War on the Economy of Paraguay," American Hemisphere Division of the Office of Economic Warfare Analysis, Board of Economic Warfare, 22 August 1942, folder: "Paraguay—Economic Conditions," Reports and Despatches from United States Missions in Latin America, Records of the Pan American Branch of the Bureau of Areas, FEA.

40. Memorandum of conversation, 5 August 1940, DS810.20 Defense/149½; despatch no. 1257, Howard to Hull, 22 August 1940, DS834.00/8-2240; despatch no. 1271, Howard to Hull, 2 September 1940, DS834.51/312½; despatch no. 1389, Howard to Hull, 4 January 1941, DS834.00/1049; letter, Frost to Armour, 28 September 1943, box no. 2, folder: "Dept. of State: Messages Sent by Wesley Frost, 1943," Wesley Frost papers, Oberlin (Ohio) College Archives (hereinafter cited as Frost MSS). Estigarribia's devotion to the cause of hemispheric solidarity did not prevent him from being simultaneously cultivated by one of the Axis powers. On 15 May 1940, Paraguay and Japan signed a trade agreement, which pointed to the exchange of Paraguayan cotton, hides, and lumber for "hardware, chemicals, machinery and other products of Japan which heretofore were practically unknown in Paraguay" ("Paraguayan Trade Commission in Japan," Boehringer, 17 May 1940, G-2 Regional File [Paraguay], no. 4000, General Records of the Office of the Director of Intelligence, Records of the War Department General and Special Staffs, RG 165, United States National Archives, Washington, D.C. [hereinafter cited as WD]).

41. Despatch no. 1274, Howard to Hull, 7 September 1940, DS711.34/20; memorandum, Duggan to Bonsal, 16 June 1941, DS834.001 Estigarribia, José Félix/47; minute, Perowne, 5 October 1940, A4097/4097/33, British Foreign Office.

42. Alberto, *Itinerario político del Paraguay*, p. 11; Bellani Nazeri, *Morínigo*, pp. 133–40; Warren, *Paraguay*, p. 331.

CHAPTER 5

1. For biographic data on Morínigo, I have relied on Bellani Nazeri, *Morínigo*, pp. 10–68, and military attaché report no. 268, Van Natta, 13 June 1941, Military Intelligence Division file no. 2271-N-155/2, General Records of the Office of the Director of Intelligence (G-2), WD.

2. Bellani Nazeri, *Morínigo*, pp. 73–91.

3. Ibid.

4. Ibid., pp. 94–97.

5. Despatch no. 1509, Schoenrich to Hull, 16 April 1941, DS834.00/1067; despatch no. 1974, Frost to Hull, 8 April 1944, DS834.00/1324; despatch no. 2134, Frost to Hull, 27 May 1944, DS834.00/1342. U.S. observers in Paraguay during the 1930s and 1940s frequently remarked on the unmistakably political deployment of Paraguay's army units—with the cavalry stationed at the interior capital and the infantry assigned to the frontiers and border regions, the reverse of orthodox defense deployment strategy.

6. Alberto, *Itinerario político del Paraguay*, pp. 9, 11–13; O. Bárcena Echeviste, *Concepción 1947: Contribución a la historia política del Paraguay* (Buenos Aires: Juan Pelligrini, 1948), pp. 134–35; Bellani Nazeri, *Morínigo*, pp. 185–87; Cardozo, *Paraguay independiente*, pp. 396–97; despatch no. 331, Frost to Hull, 27 December 1941, DS740.0011 Pacific War/1514; despatch no. 1511, Schoenrich to Hull, 19 April 1941, DS834.00/1068.

7. Despatch no. 1480, Schoenrich to Hull, 15 March 1941, DS834.00/1061; despatch no. 191, Frost to Hull, 27 September 1941, DS810.20 Defense/ 1585; despatch no. 331, Frost to Hull, 27 December 1941, DS740.0011 Pacific War/1514; despatch no. 1974, Frost to Hull, 8 April 1944, DS834.00/ 1324; despatch no. 2134, Frost to Hull, 27 May 1944, DS834.00/1342. "The Armed Forces," Army Chief of Staff Bernardo Aranda believed, "are the genuine representatives of the people, whose destiny depends on their activities and patriotism. The direction of public opinion and of collective progress fall to them by legitimate right" (quoted in despatch no. 1420, Frost to Hull, 16 October 1943, DS834.00/1250).

8. *La Tribuna* (Asunción), 26 December 1940.

9. Ibid.; *El Pais* (Asunción), 30 November 1940.

10. Alberto, *Itinerario politico del Paraguay*, p. 14; Cardozo, *Paraguay independiente*, p. 396; despatch no. 1378, Howard to Hull, 28 December 1940, DS834.00/1045; despatch no. 83, Frost to Hull, 5 July 1941, DS834.00 Revolutions/55.

11. *La Tribuna* (Asunción), 26 December 1940; Bárcena Echeviste, *Concepción 1947*, p. 124; Bellani Nazeri, *Morinigo*, pp. 281–90; Lewis, *Politics of Exile*, p. 71; Raine, *Paraguay*, pp. 261–62; despatch no. 1509, Schoenrich to Hull, 16 April 1941, DS834.00/1067; despatch no. 1708, Frost to Hull, 30 December 1943, DS834.5042/6; despatch no. 2116, Beaulac to Byrnes, 19 September 1946, DS834.5043/9-1946.

12. *La Tribuna* (Asunción), 26 December 1940; despatch no. 218, Frost to Hull, 16 October 1941, DS834.24/105; despatch no. 316, Frost to Hull, 10 August 1942, box no. 2, folder: "Dept. of State: Messages Sent by Wesley Frost, 1941–1942," Frost MSS.

13. *El Pais* (Asunción), 11 February 1941; despatch no. 161, Frost to Hull, 8 September 1941, DS834.1561/27; despatch no. 1392, Frost to Hull, 9 October 1943, DS834.515/37; "The Impact of the War on the Economy of Paraguay," American Hemisphere Division of the Office of Economic Warfare Analysis, Board of Economic Warfare, 22 August 1942, folder: "Paraguay—Economic Conditions;" Reports and Despatches from United States Missions in Latin America, Records of the Pan American Branch of the Bureau of Areas, FEA; United Nations, Department of Economic and Social Affairs, *Foreign Capital in Latin America* (New York: United Nations, 1955), pp. 129, 132; United States, Department of Commerce, Bureau of Foreign Commerce, *Investment in Paraguay: Conditions and Outlook for United States Investors* (Washington, D.C.: Government Printing Office, 1955), p. 17.

14. Despatch no. 1353, Howard to Hull, 2 December 1940, DS834.00/1042; despatch no. 96, Frost to Hull, 16 July 1941, DS834.436/17.

15. Personal letter, Higinio Morínigo to author, 12 March 1975. In responding to a series of questions, Morínigo declined to discuss his personal affiliation with the Frente de guerra.

16. G-2 report no. 5940, Van Natta to Military Intelligence Division, War De-

partment, 30 June 1941, DS834.20/114; despatch no. 80, Frost to Hull, 2 July 1941, DS811.20234/5; telegram no. 107, Frost to Hull, 18 July 1941, DS834.00/1075; despatch no. 163, Frost to Hull, 11 June 1942, DS121.5435/50; despatch no. 597, Frost to Hull, 9 December 1942, DS834.00/1163.

17. Telegram no. 109, Frost to Hull, 19 July 1941, DS834.00/1076; despatch no. 191, Frost to Hull, 27 September 1941, DS810.20 Defense/1585; despatch no. 277, Frost to Hull, 14 November 1941, DS834.24/107; despatch no. 298, Frost to Hull, 29 November 1941, DS834.24/111. Mussolini's Fascist government in Italy regarded Morínigo as a reliable friend at the start of World War II and held him in particularly high esteem for his "clean-cut fascist tendency" (State Department research and analysis report no. 3429: "Italian Fascist Documents on Italian-Paraguayan Relations," 10 November 1945, DS Lot Files).

18. Despatch no. 312, Frost to Hull, 6 December 1941, DS834.00/1093; despatch no. 367, Frost to Hull, 22 January 1942, DS800.20234/8; despatch no. 497, Frost to Hull, 30 March 1942, DS800.20234/11; despatch no. 597, Frost to Hull, 9 December 1942, DS834.00/1163; despatch no. 1369, Frost to Hull, 2 October 1943, DS834.105/18; memorandum, Dillingham to Briggs, Trueblood, Mann, 16 January 1947, DS834.002/1-1547; military attaché report no. 560, Van Natta, 2 May 1942, Army-Intelligence Project decimal file no. 413.53 Paraguay, Records of the Office of the Assistant Chief of Staff, G-2 (Intelligence), AS.

19. Despatch no. 1424, Schoenrich to Hull, 1 February 1941, DS834.911/35; despatch no. 34, Frost to Hull, 27 May 1941, DS834.00/1073; despatch no. 80, Frost to Hull, 2 July 1941, DS811.20234/5; letter, Frost to Welles, 5 July 1941, DS834.51/352; despatch no. 126, Frost to Hull, 16 August 1941, DS862.20234/44; despatch no. 371, Frost to Hull, 24 January 1942, DS834.-111/27.

20. Despatch no. 1377, Howard to Hull, 28 December 1940, DS834.51/319.

21. Willard Beaulac (United States ambassador to Paraguay, 1944–47), personal interview with author, Washington, D.C., 20 January 1975. Also see despatch no. 1974, Frost to Hull, 8 April 1944, DS834.00/1324, and memorandum, Henderson, 21 November 1944, DS834.154/10-1344; military attaché report no. 6468, Divine, 27 December 1940, Military Intelligence Division file no. 2657-N-234/30, General Records of the Office of the Director of Intelligence (G-2), WD; letter, Brickell to Perowne, 4 January 1944, AS1273/96/51, British Foreign Office. According to a 14 April 1941 *Life* magazine profile, the colorful Howard had "made the Legation a single man's paradise. Piled up in every room his visitors saw cases of Scotch. . . . The Minister . . . frowned on serious drinking before noon, and during the morning confined himself to a pink liquid identified by some visitors as pink gin. . . . After noon, however, whisky was *de riguer*. To avoid needless movement and shouting, Howard hit upon the idea of having an Indian servant follow him around at all times with a tray bearing Scotch, soda, and ice. He had only to reach out a hand for a drink."

According to Beaulac, Howard frequently worked in the nude during Asunción's oppressive summers, and occasionally received legation visitors without bothering to dress.

22. Letter, Welles to Roosevelt, 7 February 1941, DS834.0011/7; memorandum, Donovan to Hull, 15 May 1941, DS834.0011/23; letter, Soler to Welles, 28 July 1941, DS834.0011/42.

23. Despatch no. 1509, Schoenrich to Hull, 16 April 1941, DS834.00/1067; enclosure to despatch no. 1, Frost to Hull, 2 May 1941, DS834.51/339; telegram no. 62, Welles to Frost, 23 July 1941, DS834.51/348; draft letters, Welles to Frost, August 1941, DS834.00/1081; letter, Pierson to Collado, 16 December 1941, DS834.51/367; enclosure to letter, Frost to Armour, 28 September 1943, box no. 2, folder: "Dept. of State: Messages Sent by Wesley Frost, 1943," Frost MSS. "I should think," a State Department official remarked, "that the Paraguayan Government would see a connection between the recent action of the Bolivian Government in making it quite clear to the world that Bolivia will in no sense be a refuge for pro-Axis elements and the initiation by the United States of a very broad program of cooperation with Bolivia . . . with respect to Bolivia's transportation needs . . . agriculture and mining. The Bolivian Government made Bolivia safe for democracy and this enabled the United States to proceed with a long-term plan of construction."

24. Despatch no. 1509, Schoenrich to Hull, 16 April 1941, DS834.00/1067; telegram no. 44, Hull to Frost, 7 June 1941, DS834.20/108; memorandum of conversation, 23 July 1941, DS834.20/112; draft letter, Duggan to Frost, n.d., DS834.00/1073; memorandum, Wilson to Hull, 20 September 1941, DS834.24/93.

25. Adolf Augustus Berle, *Navigating the Rapids, 1918–1971: From the Papers of Adolf A. Berle,* ed. Beatrice Bishop Berle and Travis Beal Jacobs (New York: Harcourt Brace Jovanovich, Inc., 1973), p. 398.

26. For a detailed, albeit noninterpretive, description of the Rio Conference, see Michael J. Francis, *The Limits of Hegemony: United States Relations with Argentina and Chile during World War II* (Notre Dame, Ind.: University of Notre Dame Press, 1977), chap. 3.

27. McCann, *Brazilian-American Alliance,* pp. 5–8, 112, 250–69, 304–7; *FRUS,* 1942, 5:45, memorandum: "Progress in Carrying Out Economic Arrangements Discussed at the Rio Meeting," Collado to Welles, 28 February 1942.

28. Sumner Welles, *The Time for Decision* (Cleveland and New York: World Publishing Co., 1945), pp. 223–35; Potash, *Army and Politics in Argentina,* pp. 116–19, 125, 143, 160–70; *FRUS,* 1942, 5:30–32, telegram no. 27, Welles to Hull, 19 January 1942.

29. *New York Times,* 22 July 1942.

30. Despatch no. 312, Frost to Hull, 6 December 1941, DS834.00/1093; despatch no. 331, Frost to Hull, 27 December 1941, DS740.0011 Pacific War/1514; despatch no. 163, Frost to Hull, 11 June 1942, DS121.5434/50.

31. Enclosure to despatch no. 91, Frost to Hull, 22 May 1942, DS740.0011 European War 1939/21989.
32. Memorandum: "Paraguayan Request for Export-Import Bank Assistance," Collado to Welles, 11 April 1942, DS834.51/397.

CHAPTER 6

1. The following account of Morínigo's economic-development program is drawn largely from "The Impact of the War on the Economy of Paraguay," American Hemisphere Division of the Office of Economic Warfare Analysis, Board of Economic Warfare, 22 August 1942, folder: "Paraguay—Economic Conditions," Reports and Despatches from United States Missions in Latin America, Records of the Pan American Branch of the Bureau of Areas, FEA; despatch no. 741 and enclosure, Frost to Hull, 29 January 1943, DS834.50/62; "Report of the Agricultural Bank of Paraguay," enclosure to despatch no. 580, Beaulac to Stettinius, 22 February 1945, DS834.51/2-2245; economic report no. 22, Fernandez, 29 March 1944, G-2 Regional File (Paraguay), General Records of the Office of the Director of Intelligence (G-2), WD; "Industrial Plan for Paraguay," Servicio Técnico Interamericano de Cooperación Agrícola, 1 April 1944, box no. 2, folder: "Writings in English, c.1942–1944," Frost MSS; Raine, *Paraguay*, chaps. 7, 9; U.S., Department of Commerce, *Investment in Paraguay*, p. 15.
2. Telegram no. 34, Welles to Frost, 6 February 1942, DS834.51/379; memorandum: "Paraguayan Request for Export-Import Bank Assistance," Collado to Welles, 11 April 1942, DS834.51/397; "Paraguayan Summary," sole enclosure to letter, Frost to Armour, 28 September 1943, box no. 2, folder: "Dept. of State: Messages Sent by Wesley Frost, 1943," Frost MSS (hereinafter cited as " 'Paraguayan Summary,' Frost MSS"). "The only possible way of getting certain of these development and highway projects organized and moving forward on a somewhat efficient basis," Collado concluded, "is to establish in Paraguay a development corporation along the lines of that established in Haiti and that being established in Ecuador, that is with an effective United States manager to carry the load."
3. Despatch no. 535, Frost to Hull, 10 April 1942, DS834.51/389; memorandum, Woodward to Dreier, Bonsal, Collado, Duggan, 27 April 1942, DS834.51/394; "Paraguayan Summary," Frost MSS. "I . . . urge as strongly as possible that a generous measure of economic help be announced within the next month or six weeks," Frost wrote. "The problem is not an economic one (or at least only secondarily so). It is definitely political. The officials of our Government who are entrusted with its solution should not be economic but political officials. They should think not primarily in terms of a rational long-distance scientific plan for the development of Paraguay but in terms of a present international exigency." "It is in my judgment folly for us to confine ourselves in Paraguay to a program which a scientific economist or a New England conscience would regard as proper."
4. Telegram no. 179, Frost to Welles, 3 May 1942, DS834.50/24; "Paraguayan

Summary," Frost MSS. The military faction eventually succeeded in ousting Argaña and the Tiempistas from the government in March 1944. Four months earlier, in December 1943, nationalist revolutionaries had overthrown the corrupt Peñaranda regime in neighboring Bolivia. The new Bolivian government was a coalition of young authoritarian nationalist army officers led by Major Gualberto Villarroel and civilian intellectuals of Víctor Paz Estenssoro's Nationalist Revolutionary Movement, an urban middle-class reform movement which advocated fundamental social reforms and the nationalization of Bolivia's tin mines and public utilities. Viewing the new regime as "profascist" and "under Nazi influence," the United States refused to grant it diplomatic recognition and requested that the other Latin American nations follow a similar policy (*FRUS*, 1943, 5:539–43, telegram no. 2094, Boal to Hull, 29 December 1943; *FRUS*, 1944, 7:431, circular telegram, Hull to United States Diplomatic Representatives in Brazil, Chile, Colombia, Ecuador, Paraguay, Peru, and Uruguay, 10 January 1944). When Argaña conformed to the United States request, the military group was incensed and labeled the decision "subservience" to the United States. Then, in February 1944, an extreme nationalist military group, led by General Edelmiro Farrell and Colonel Juan Perón, seized power in Argentina, and the United States attempted to forge another hemispheric diplomatic quarantine of nonrecognition. When Argaña withheld formal Paraguayan recognition from the new Argentine government, the outraged military faction accused him of "slavish acquiescence" to the United States and persuaded Morínigo to remove the foreign minister and his civilian colleagues from the cabinet (telegram no. 173, Frost to Hull, 24 March 1944, DS834.00/1303; military attaché report no. 1984, McAdams, 21 March 1944, G-2 Regional File [Paraguay], no. 3020, General Records of the Office of the Director of Intelligence [G-2], WD; naval attaché report no. R-43-44, 24 March 1944, G-2 Regional File [Paraguay], no. 3110, General Records of the Office of the Director of Intelligence [G-2], WD).

5. R. W. Hebard and Company.

6. Letter, Welles to Velazquez, 5 May 1942, DS834.61A/10A; despatch no. 260, Frost to Hull, 22 July 1942, DS834.514/105; letter, Pierson to Duggan, 5 August 1942, DS834.154/106; letter, Duggan to Pierson, 6 August 1942, DS834.154/106; "Paraguayan Summary," Frost MSS.

7. Memorandum, Bonsal to Welles, 11 June 1943, DS834.24/410; memorandum of conversation, 11 June 1943, DS834.24/515; letter, Frost to Duggan, 19 August 1943, DS834.24/497; letter, Frost to Duggan, 11 September 1943, DS834.24/509; "Paraguayan Summary," Frost MSS; personal letter, Higinio Morínigo to author, 12 March 1975.

8. Conn and Fairchild, *Western Hemisphere*, pp. 251–52, 258–59; Gardner, *Economic Aspects of New Deal Diplomacy*, p. 62.

9. *FRUS*, 1942, 6:646, telegram no. 225, Frost to Hull, 22 May 1942; *FRUS*, 1942, 6:650–52, telegram no. 258, Frost to Hull, 11 June 1942; "Paraguayan Summary," Frost MSS.

10. Memorandum, Bacon to Bonsal, Duggan, 22 October 1942, DS834.7962/21; memorandum of conversation, 5 November 1942, DS834.7962/28; memorandum, Welles to Bonsal, 21 February 1943, DS834.7962/44; *FRUS*, 1942, 6:650–52, telegram no. 258, Frost to Hull, 11 June 1942; "Paraguayan Summary," Frost MSS.

11. Despatch no. 184, Beaulac to Hull, 28 October 1944, DS834.796/10-2844; enclosure to despatch no. 1284, Beaulac to Byrnes, 21 November 1945, DS834.20 Missions/11-2145; despatch no. 1737, Beaulac to Byrnes, 23 May 1946, DS834.796/5-2346; memorandum, Briggs, 27 June 1946, DS813.796 TACA/6-2746.

12. Airgram no. A-281, Hull to United States Embassy, Asunción, 10 July 1943, DS834.6363/144B; memorandum, Dawson to Wright, Bonsal, Townsend, Collado, Duggan, 26 August 1943, DS834.6363/163; telegram no. 616, Frost to Hull, 16 November 1943, DS834.6363/176; despatch no. 1624, Frost to Hull, 9 December 1943, DS834.6363/186; telegram no. 50, Stettinius to United States Embassy, Asunción, 18 February 1944, DS834.6363/200; memorandum, Wright to Bonsal, 23 February 1944, DS834.6363/202; enclosure to despatch no. 93, Beaulac to Hull, 7 October 1944, DS834.6363/10-744; memorandum of conversation, 17 October 1944, DS834.6363/10-1744. Emphasis in original.

13. Gardner, *Economic Aspects of New Deal Diplomacy*, pp. 111, 208.

14. Companía Internacional de Teléfonos, a subsidiary of Siemens-Halske.

15. Telegram no. 594, Beaulac to Hull, 17 October 1944, DS834.74/10-1744; enclosure to despatch no. 16,475, Berger to Hull, 27 October 1944, DS834.-74/10-2744; despatch no. 590, Beaulac to Stettinius, 27 February 1945, DS834.75/2-2745; telegram no. 502, Beaulac to Byrnes, 9 October 1945, DS834.75/10-945; enclosure to despatch no. 1537, Beaulac to Byrnes, 19 March 1946, DS834.75/3-1946; despatch no. 1810, Beaulac to Byrnes, 14 July 1946, DS834.75/6-1446. For the changed political climate in Paraguay that by 1946 made Morínigo amenable to a telecommunications contract with a United States corporation, see below, chap. 8.

16. Despatch no. 1740, Frost to Hull, 15 January 1944, DS834.50/73; despatch no. 1822, Frost to Hull, 15 February 1944, DS834.50/76; enclosure to despatch no. 1825, Frost to Hull, 18 February 1944, DS834.50/77.

17. Letter, Frost to Dawson, 1 February 1944, box no. 2, folder: "Dept. of State: Messages Sent by Wesley Frost, 1944," Frost MSS; "Industrial Plan for Paraguay," Servicio Técnico Interamericano de Cooperación Agrícola, 1 April 1944, box no. 2, folder: "Writings in English, c.1942–1944," Frost MSS; despatch no. 2130, Frost to Hull, 26 May 1944, DS834.50/79; *Inter-American*, no. 4 (December 1945), p. 39.

18. Enclosure to despatch no. 2360, Reed to Hull, 11 August 1944, DS710.Development Commission/8-1144.

CHAPTER 7

1. Woolf, "Did a Fascist Economic System Exist?" pp. 145–46.

2. Laurence Duggan, *The Americas: The Search for Hemispheric Security* (New York: Henry Holt & Co., 1949), pp. 147–48.
3. Green, *Containment of Latin America,* pp. 113–21.
4. Dozer, *Are We Good Neighbors?* p. 122.
5. United Nations, *Foreign Capital in Latin America,* p. 12; Behrendt, *Inter-American Economic Relations,* p. 87.
6. *FRUS,* 1947, 8:267, memorandum, Ohmans, 12 June 1947.
7. United Nations, *Foreign Capital in Latin America,* pp. 12–13; *FRUS,* 1948, 9:251, enclosure to circular airgram DS-4, Acting Secretary of State to Diplomatic Representatives in Certain American Republics, 13 October 1948; Dozer, *Are We Good Neighbors?* pp. 247–48.
8. Quoted in Green, *Containment of Latin America,* p. 139.
9. "Memorandum on Post-War Planning for Latin America," Bidwell, 23 June 1942, folder: "Post-War Planning," Central Files, OIAA.
10. "Estimates of Import Requirements, Three-Year Period, Post-Hostilities," Foreign Economic Development Staff of the Office of Economic Programs, 20 December 1944, folder: "Latin America (Exports-Imports)," Reports on Foreign Economic Conditions (Geographic File), 1942–1945, Office of the Administrator, FEA.
11. Spruille Braden, "Latin-American Industrialization and Foreign Trade," in *Industrialization of Latin America,* ed. Lloyd J. Hughlett (New York and London: McGraw-Hill Book Co., Inc., 1946), pp. 490–91.
12. Quoted in Dozer, *Are We Good Neighbors?* p. 219.
13. *FRUS,* 1946, 11:534, telegram no. 2693, Byrnes to Berle, 30 November 1945.
14. Of the more than $28 billion in United States foreign aid allocated between July 1945 and July 1950, Latin America received $514 million, or 1.8 percent. Dozer, *Are We Good Neighbors?* pp. 239, 241–42.
15. Braden, "Latin-American Industrialization and Foreign Trade," p. 489.
16. United States, Department of State, *Private Enterprise in the Development of the Americas: An Address by Assistant Secretary Braden before the Executives' Club of Chicago, September 13, 1946,* Inter-American Series, no. 32 (Washington, D.C.: Government Printing Office, 1946), pp. 3, 5. Also quoted in Green, *Containment of Latin America,* p. 262.
17. Dozer, *Are We Good Neighbors?* p. 244.
18. Ibid., p. 242; Pike, "Corporatism and Latin American–United States Relations," p. 151.
19. *FRUS,* 1945, 9:73, memorandum of conversation, 29 January 1945.
20. United States, Department of State, *Report of the Delegation of the United States of America to the Inter-American Conference on Problems of War and Peace, Mexico City, Mexico, February 21–March 8, 1945* (Washington, D.C.: Government Printing Office, 1946), pp. 277–80.
21. Duggan, *The Americas,* pp. 116–17; Pike, "Corporatism and Latin American–United States Relations," pp. 150–51.
22. Quoted in Green, *Containment of Latin America,* p. 141.
23. *FRUS,* 1948, 9:198–99, enclosure no. 2 to unnumbered circular instruction,

Marshall to Diplomatic Representatives in the American Republics, 21 June 1948. During 1946, the State Department was keeping a close watch on reported Russian offers to "former Proclaimed List nationals" in southern South America of "exclusive distribution and selling rights for South America of 'Russian Made' pharmaceuticals, chemicals, and dyestuffs" (*FRUS,* 1946, 11:85, circular airgram, Acheson to Diplomatic Representatives in the American Republics, 3 December 1946).

24. United States, Department of State, *Report of the Delegation of the United States of America to the Inter-American Conference on Problems of War and Peace,* pp. 120–24, 277–80.

25. "Special Area Considerations of the Pan American Branch," Foreign Economic Development Staff of the Office of Economic Programs, 21 December 1944, folder: "Latin America (Exports-Imports)," Reports on Foreign Economic Conditions (Geographic File), 1942–1945, Records of the Office of the Administrator, FEA. According to this document, "the prime end to be served by" the Foreign Economic Administration's Latin American "policy is the maintenance of economic, political and military security through (a) Assurance of access to raw materials essential for military and industrial purposes; (b) The promotion of a high level of foreign trade; and (c) Reduction in some instances of the drain on domestic sub-soil resources in short supply."

26. Memorandum, Chalmers, 23 August 1945, DS834.51/8-2345.

27. Weber, *Varieties of Fascism,* p. 61.

28. See, for example, Skidmore, *Politics in Brazil,* pp. 39–41.

29. Green, *Containment of Latin America,* pp. 217, 234; Blanksten, *Perón's Argentina,* pp. 406–8.

30. *FRUS,* 1945, 9:426, letter, Cabot to Briggs, 17 November 1945.

31. *FRUS,* 1945, 9:392, telegram no. 1498, Braden to Byrnes, 11 July 1945.

32. Telegram no. 1871, Braden to Byrnes, 17 August 1945, DS123 Braden, Spruille; despatch no. 398, Braden to Byrnes, 28 July 1945, DS123 Braden, Spruille; telegram no. 1993, Braden to Byrnes, 28 August 1945, DS711.35/8-2845; Alexander, *Perón Era,* pp. 47, 204; Oscar Edmund Smith, *Yankee Diplomacy: U.S. Intervention in Argentina* (Dallas, Tex.: Southern Methodist University Press, 1953), p. 143. Braden recounts his experiences in *Diplomats and Demagogues: The Memoirs of Spruille Braden* (New Rochelle, N.Y.: Arlington House, 1971).

33. Smith, *Yankee Diplomacy,* pp. 144–45.

34. *FRUS,* 1945, 9:422–23, telegram no. 2598, Cabot to Byrnes, 19 October 1945; *FRUS,* 1945, 9:430, letter, Cabot to Briggs, 17 November 1945. "The old families here," said Cabot, "make New York bankers sound like William Z. Foster."

35. *FRUS,* 1946, 11:201, telegram no. 430, Cabot to Byrnes, 8 February 1946; *FRUS,* 1945, 9:429, letter, Cabot to Briggs, 17 November 1945; *FRUS,* 1945, 9:436, telegram no. 3033, Cabot to Byrnes, 4 December 1945; United States, Department of State, *Consultation among the American Republics with*

Respect to the Argentine Situation (Washington, D.C.: Government Printing Office, 1946).

36. Despatch no. 546, Chapin to Stettinius, 13 March 1945, DS832.00/3-1345; despatch no. 2510, Berle to Byrnes, 22 August 1945, DS832.00/8-2245; despatch no. 2611, Chapin to Byrnes, 27 August 1945, DS832.00/8-2745; memorandum, Mein to Chalmers, 31 August 1945, DS832.00/8-3145; Skidmore, *Politics in Brazil,* pp. 48–52, 56–57, 59–60, 67; McCann, *Brazilian-American Alliance,* pp. 468–71.

37. Memorandum, Harrison to Chalmers, 27 January 1945, DS832.00/1-2745; despatch no. 857, Chapin to Stettinius, 4 April 1945, DS832.00/4-445; enclosure to despatch no. 2103, Berle to Byrnes, 19 July 1945, DS832.00/7-1945; memorandum, Yenchius to Mein, Harrison, Braddock, Chalmers, 30 July 1945, DS832.00/7-1945; McCann, *Brazilian-American Alliance,* pp. 453, 465; Skidmore, *Politics in Brazil,* p. 60.

38. Skidmore, *Politics in Brazil,* p. 51; *FRUS,* 1945, 9:717, economic report no. 28, Berle to Stettinius, 29 January 1945; *FRUS,* 1945, 9:723, no. 7571, Clayton to Berle, 5 October 1945; *FRUS,* 1946, 11:523–25, telegram no. 2599, Byrnes to Berle, 10 November 1945; *FRUS,* 1946, 11:527, telegram no. 3411, Berle to Byrnes, 13 November 1945.

39. Memorandum, Braddock and Mein to Chalmers, 21 September 1945, DS832.00/9-345; McCann, *Brazilian-American Alliance,* pp. 471–74, 476.

40. Berle, *Navigating the Rapids,* p. 548.

41. Telegram no. 3008, Berle to Truman, Braden, 29 September 1945, DS832.00/9-2945; enclosure to letter, Rambo to Berle, 5 October 1945, DS832.00/10-545; *Correio da manhã* (Rio de Janeiro), 30 September 1945.

42. McCann, *Brazilian-American Alliance,* pp. 443–45, 449, 476–84. U.S. intervention should, of course, be interpreted as merely one of several factors in a complex equation of events that led to the overthrow of Vargas. In the end, Vargas's own maneuverings provided the occasion for his removal. Throughout October, the dictator continued to issue enigmatic public statements which seemed to offer encouragement to his political supporters in their campaign to promote his continuance in office. Meanwhile, Vargas's lieutenants were actively organizing a new Brazilian Labor Party. Then, on October 25, Vargas announced that he would appoint his brother to the post of chief of police of the Federal District, a move that lent further credence to suspicions that a preservative internal coup was in the offing. Four days later, on October 29, the army—nervous over the prospect that the new Brazilian Labor Party would provide Vargas with an independent power base of militant labor support similar to that which Perón was simultaneously forging in Argentina, and desiring Brazil's future international acceptance as a coequal "democratic" partner by her U.S. and European wartime allies—quietly deposed the dictator on behalf of "democratic processes."

43. Alexander, *Perón Era,* pp. 154–69; Dozer, *Are We Good Neighbors?* p. 296. "We have transformed the economic order and established economic so-

cialism," Perón declared in 1950; "that is, whereas capitalism put the national economy at its service, we now put capital at the service of the national economy."

44. Skidmore, *Politics in Brazil,* pp. 66, 69–70. Eleven days after his electoral victory, Dutra announced publicly: "Economic liberty will perhaps be the principal point in my governmental program. . . . Economic liberty must be a reality not only within our frontiers and for internal commerce but also for foreign commerce. The increase of imports is indispensable for the raising of our standard of living. I do not agree with the permanent protection of industries which do not have real economic possibilities and only exist by lowering the standard of living. Consequently, I believe it necessary that Brazil must offer all guarantees to foreign capital in order that it may contribute considerably to the development of Brazil. I make no distinction between foreign and national enterprises once they are both working for the economic progress of my country. We should receive with all satisfaction and on an equal basis with national capital, all foreign capital desiring to collaborate with us. . . . I am fundamentally against unlimited extension of the power of the state. . . . The state cannot fail to see that its interference in economic matters lessens the scope of action of private initiative, and it should not invade this field by means of the direction or acquisition of industrial or agricultural enterprises. The state should only undertake that which private initiative cannot accomplish. . . . I see in Pan-Americanism the only real form of efficient defense and real progress for the American continent. I am a firm believer in the continuation of the policy of strict collaboration with the United States of America in favor of peace and continental harmony within the democratic regime" (quoted in airgram no. A-890, Baruch [Lisbon] to Byrnes, 13 December 1945, DS832.00/12-1345).

CHAPTER 8

1. Despatch no. 1153-A, Montgomery to Hull, 8 July 1943, DS834.911/47; despatch no. 1345, Frost to Hull, 24 September 1943, DS810.74/1014; memorandum, Keeley to Duggan, Bonsal, 1 April 1944, DS740.00115 European War (1939)/9027; despatch no. 2290, Reed to Hull, 20 July 1944, DS862.-20210 Stagni, Pablo (Major)/7-2044; memorandum, Division of American Republic Affairs, 9 August 1944, DS862.20210, Stagni, Pablo (Major)/8-944; enclosure to despatch no. 1952, Frost to Hull, 1 April 1944, box no. 2, folder: "Dept. of State: Messages Sent by Wesley Frost, 1944," Frost MSS; despatch no. 37, N. O. W. Steward to Eden, 16 August 1944, AS4743/1220/30, British Foreign Office. Several Nazi war criminals, including former SS official Adolf Eichmann and Auschwitz concentration-camp physician Josef Mengele, relocated to Paraguay after World War II. See *New York Times,* 23 December 1967, and *Washington Post,* 3 March 1976.

2. Despatch no. 1443, Frost to Hull, 23 October 1943, DS834.00/1252.

3. Paraguayan women did not receive the franchise until 1963.

4. Despatch no. 703, Frost to Hull, 12 January 1943, DS834.00/1181; despatch

no. 744, Frost to Hull, 25 January 1943, DS834.00/1187; despatch no. 872, Frost to Hull, 18 March 1943, DS834.00/1210.

5. Despatch no. 948, Frost to Hull, 13 April 1943, DS834.20/134; despatch no. 1420, Frost to Hull, 16 October 1943, DS834.00/1250; despatch no. 1928, Frost to Hull, 25 March 1944, DS834.00/1313; telegram no. 187, Beaulac to Byrnes, 3 May 1946, DS862.20210/5-346; *FRUS*, 1944, 7:1498–99, despatch no. 2121, Frost to Hull, 23 May 1944; *FRUS*, 1945, 9:1279, telegram no. 86, Grew to Beaulac, 11 January 1945; *FRUS*, 1945, 9:1281, telegram no. 101, Beaulac to Stettinius, 7 February 1945; *FRUS*, 1946, 11:1197, despatch no. 1739, Beaulac to Byrnes, 24 May 1946; *New York Times,* 18 May 1946.

6. Despatch no. 1974, Frost to Hull, 8 April 1944, DS834.00/1324.

7. Ibid.

8. Ibid.; despatch no. 2109, Frost to Hull, 20 May 1944, DS834.00/1340; letter, Frost to Hull, 4 March 1944, DS810.20 Defense/3-444. Emphasis in original.

9. Despatch no. 743, Beaulac to Stettinius, 27 April 1945, DS834.00/4-2745; despatch no. 922, Beaulac to Byrnes, 7 July 1945, DS711.00/7-745; despatch no. 1067, Beaulac to Byrnes, 4 September 1945, DS123 Beaulac, Willard.

10. Despatch no. 922, Beaulac to Byrnes, 7 July 1945, DS711.00/7-745; enclosure no. 2 to despatch no. 1066, Beaulac to Byrnes, 4 September 1945, DS123 Beaulac, Willard; despatch no. 1119, Beaulac to Byrnes, 24 September 1945, DS834.00/9-2445. Also see Carlos Borche, *Campos de concentración en América (Misión en Paraguay)* (Montevideo: Ediciones Patrocinadas por el Comité Nacional de Ayuda al Pueblo Paraguayo, 1945), pp. 129–30. "The economic problems of today . . . can be achieved [*sic*] only through cooperation among democratic peoples," Beaulac told the Paraguayan cabinet and other government officials in an address before the Paraguayan-American Cultural Center on 3 September 1945. "All nations must be assured of access to the world's products. To this end, tariffs must be progressively scaled down. Autarchy must be renounced. Equality of treatment to all nations must be the rule. Isolationism, political and economic, must give way to cooperation."

11. Despatch no. 1119, Beaulac to Byrnes, 24 September 1945, DS834.00/9-2445. Beaulac recalls his Paraguayan experiences in *Career Ambassador* (New York: Macmillan Co., 1951), chaps. 26 and 27.

12. Despatch no. 346, Beaulac to Stettinius, 13 December 1944, DS834.00/12-1344; telegram no. 238, Grew to Beaulac, 11 July 1945, DS834.00/7-545; telegram no. 380, Beaulac to Byrnes, 12 July 1945, DS834.00/7-1245; despatch no. 1119, Beaulac to Byrnes, 24 September 1945, DS834.00/9-2445; telegram no. 633, Beaulac to Byrnes, 24 December 1945, DS711.34/12-2445; despatch no. 1358, Beaulac to Byrnes, 26 December 1945, DS711.34/12-2645; telegram no. 390, Acheson to Beaulac, 28 December 1945, DS711.34/12-2645.

13. Despatch no. 2293, Reed to Hull, 19 July 1944, DS834.4212/7-1944; telegram no. 657, Beaulac to Hull, 22 November 1944, DS834.00/11-2244; despatch no. 271, Beaulac to Hull, 25 November 1944, DS834.00/11-2544; telegram no. 725, Beaulac to Stettinius, 28 December 1944, DS834.00/12-

2844; despatch no. 743, Beaulac to Stettinius, 27 April 1945, DS834.00/4-2745; Alberto, *Itinerario político del Paraguay*, p. 19.

14. Military attaché report no. R-5-46, Pearson, 7 January 1946, area file no. XL 36602, OSS; memorandum of conversation, 15 January 1946, DS711.34/1-1546; telegram no. 100, Beaulac to Byrnes, 4 March 1946, DS834.00/3-446; despatch no. 1608, Beaulac to Byrnes, 11 April 1946, DS711.34/4-1146.

15. Telegram no. 254, Beaulac to Byrnes, 9 June 1946, DS834.00/6-946; telegram no. 257, Beaulac to Byrnes, 11 June 1946, DS834.00/6-1146; telegram no. 305, Beaulac to Byrnes, 9 July 1946, DS834.918/7-946; telegram no. 331, Beaulac to Byrnes, 19 July 1946, DS834.00/7-1946; telegram no. 341, Beaulac to Byrnes, 23 July 1946, DS834.00/7-2346; telegram no. 345, Beaulac to Byrnes, 26 July 1946, DS834.00/7-2646; despatch no. 1945, Beaulac to Byrnes, 27 July 1946, DS834.00/7-2746; despatch no. 1953, Beaulac to Byrnes, 31 July 1946, DS834.00/7-3146; *La Tribuna* (Asunción), 26 July 1946.

16. Telegram no. 353, Beaulac to Byrnes, 31 July 1946, DS834.00/7-3146; despatch no. 2067, Beaulac to Byrnes, 4 September 1946, DS834.5043/9-446; despatch no. 2307, Beaulac to Byrnes, 5 December 1946, DS834.00/12-546; despatch no. 2354, Beaulac to Byrnes, 26 December 1946, DS834.00B/12-2646; despatch no. 2424, Beaulac to Marshall, 20 January 1947, DS834.00/1-2047.

17. Despatch no. 2395, Beaulac to Marshall, 11 January 1947, DS834.00/1-1147; telegram no. 11, Beaulac to Marshall, 13 January 1947, DS834.00/1-1347; memorandum, Dillingham to Mann, 15 January 1947, DS834.00/1-1547; despatch no. 2424, Beaulac to Marshall, 20 January 1947, DS834.00/1-2047.

18. Despatch no. 2140, Beaulac to Byrnes, 28 September 1946, DS834.796/9-2846.

19. Despatch no. 1974, Frost to Hull, 8 April 1944, DS834.00/1324; memorandum, Dillingham to Mann, 22 August 1946, DS834.00/7-1246; memorandum, Dillingham to Mann, 27 August 1946, DS711.3411/8-2746; despatch no. 2307, Beaulac to Byrnes, 5 December 1946, DS834.00/12-546; despatch no. 2336, Beaulac to Byrnes, 17 December 1946, DS834.00/12-1746.

20. Despatch no. 1119, Beaulac to Byrnes, 24 September 1945, DS834.00/9-2445; memorandum, Dillingham to Mann, 22 August 1946, DS834.00/7-1246.

21. Telegram no. 409, Beaulac to Byrnes, 12 September 1946, DS611.3431/9-1246; enclosure to despatch no. 2514, Trueblood to Marshall, 3 March 1947, DS611.3431/3-347.

22. Enclosure to despatch no. 2535, Trueblood to Marshall, 12 March 1947, DS834.00/3-1247; despatch no. 2671, Trueblood to Marshall, 28 May 1947, DS834.00/5-2847; despatch no. 2969, Warren to Marshall, 10 November 1947, DS834.50/11-1047; *La Razón* (Asunción), 22 April 1947.

23. Despatch no. 2405, Beaulac to Marshall, 15 January 1947, DS834.00/1-1547.

24. Telegram no. 11, Beaulac to Marshall, 13 January 1947, DS834.00/1-1347; despatch no. 2434, Beaulac to Marshall, 21 January 1947, DS834.00/1-2147; despatch no. 2462, Reed to Marshall, 5 February 1947, DS834.00/2-547; telegram no. 332, Trueblood to Marshall, 20 June 1947, DS834.00/6-2047.

25. Telegram no. 137, Trueblood to Marshall, 21 March 1947, DS834.00/3-2147; despatch no. 2630, Trueblood to Marshall, 7 May 1947, DS834.00/5-747; despatch no. 2825, Trueblood to Marshall, 27 August 1947, DS834.00/8-2747. "Whereas Perón may have 500,000 *descamisados* [shirtless ones] to support him," Morínigo declared two days after the civil war began, "I have 180,000 *py nandi* to support me" (despatch no. 2532, Trueblood to Marshall, 10 March 1947, DS834.00/3-1047; despatch no. 2660, Trueblood to Marshall, 23 May 1947, DS834.00/5-2347).

26. Despatch no. 2722, Trueblood to Marshall, 24 June 1947, DS834.00/6-2447.

27. Despatch no. 2825, Trueblood to Marshall, 27 August 1947, DS834.00/8-2747; despatch no. 2844, Hoyt to Marshall, 8 September 1947, DS834.00/9-847; Bárcena Echeviste, *Concepción 1947,* p. 273; Bourne, *Political Leaders of Latin America,* pp. 110–12. Early in the 1947 civil war, the Colorados asked the governments of the United States, Argentina, and Brazil for aircraft, tanks, and firearms, claiming that the Morínigo regime was being attacked by a Communist-Febrerista-Liberal "triple alliance" dominated by "servants of Moscow" and dedicated to the implantation of a Communist regime in Paraguay and that as a result, the Paraguayan government should be supplied with the arms necessary to defend "hemispheric security" against "the bloody designs of Stalinist imperialism" (telegram, Chaves to Marshall, 17 March 1947, DS834.00/3-1747; despatch no. 2825, Trueblood to Marshall, 27 August 1947, DS834.00/8-2747; Juan Natalicio González and Víctor Morínigo, *Bajo las bombas del malón* [Asunción: Editorial Guarania, 1947], pp. 7–8).

The extent of Communist influence on the rebel side was a matter of considerable interest to the Truman administration, which quickly dispatched a special agent of the new Central Intelligence Agency, Collins D. Almon, to collect information on Communist involvement in the civil war. Almon and other U.S. sources reported that while the revolt was "far from a Communist-dominated rebellion," Communists were exerting "considerable influence in the rebel ranks." An international Communist brigade of between 250 and 350 Argentine, Bolivian, Brazilian, and Paraguayan Communists, wearing special hammer-and-sickle arm bands, was extremely active in the fighting. In April 1947, a Soviet agent was apprehended in Asunción while engaged in making hand grenades for a rebel fifth column in the capital. Nevertheless, despite a strong recommendation by Ambassador Beaulac that Morínigo be permitted to purchase arms from private suppliers in the United States, the State Department eventually decided that the "Communist danger" was not "sufficiently certain or immediate" to justify the public or private supply of U.S. arms to the Paraguayan government's forces. "We may soon have to take the initiative in working out a program to combat Communist tactics in this Hemisphere," Undersecretary of State Braden concluded, "but the program should . . . be an inter-American one" (memorandum, Beaulac to Marshall, Braden, Clayton, Briggs, 13 June 1947, DS834.00/6-1347; despatch no. 2818, Trueblood to

Marshall, 25 August 1947, DS834.00/8-2547; *FRUS*, 1947, 8:981–82, memorandum, Braden to Acheson, 23 April 1947; *FRUS*, 1947, 8:995–96, despatch no. 2853, Hoyt to Marshall, 9 September 1947; for details regarding the Soviet agent, Nicolai Riline, see Edgar Ynsfran, *La irrupción moscovita en la Marina Paraguaya* [Asunción: privately printed, 1947], p. 17).

Argentina's Perón regime, after an initial period of hesitation to determine which side was most likely to emerge victorious, secretly funneled aircraft, arms, and ammunition to Morínigo and the Colorados. Indeed, during the final rebel assault on Asunción in August 1947, rebel participants reported that the last-minute appearance of "powerful new automatic arms" among the capital's defenders, presumably supplied by Perón, proved decisive in the Colorado victory (telegram no. 337, Trueblood to Marshall, 23 June 1947, DS834.7965/6-2347; despatch no. 2766, Trueblood to Marshall, 16 July 1947, DS734.35/7-1647; telegram no. 479, Trueblood to Marshall, 21 August 1947, DS834.00/8-2147; despatch no. 2823, Trueblood to Marshall, 25 August 1947, DS834.00/8-2547; Bárcena Echeviste, *Concepción 1947,* p. 257).

The Uruguayan government, on the other hand, actively channeled arms, foodstuffs, and medical supplies to the rebel forces (telegram no. 464, Trueblood to Marshall, 18 August 1947, DS834.00/8-1847; despatch no. 979, Sparks to Marshall, 21 August 1947, DS834.00/8-2147; telegram no. 363, Briggs to Marshall, DS834.00/8-2347).

No evidence of Brazilian involvement on behalf of either side has come to light.

28. *FRUS,* 1947, 8:65–67, memorandum of conversation, 27 August 1947.
29. Lewis, *Politics of Exile,* p. 80; Leo B. Lott, *Venezuela and Paraguay: Political Modernity and Tradition in Conflict* (New York: Holt, Rinehart & Winston, Inc., 1972), p. 272. In September 1947, the archbishop of the Paraguayan Catholic Church issued a nationwide pastoral letter which charged that "robbery, looting, rape, assassination and other atrocities, in a scale never before witnessed, are being committed throughout the republic" (see despatch no. 2846, Trueblood to Marshall, 17 September 1947, DS834.00/9-1747).
30. Despatch no. 93, Warren to Marshall, 17 February 1948, DS834.00/2-1748; *New York Times,* 16 February 1948.

CONCLUSION

1. See tables 1, 3, 6, and 8, above.
2. Ibid.
3. Despatch no. 821, Frost to Hull, 26 February 1943, DS834.51A/106.
4. For a valuable analysis of liberal imperialism as the motive force of nineteenth-century British and twentieth-century United States foreign policy, see David P. Calleo and Benjamin M. Rowland, *America and the World Political Economy: Atlantic Dreams and National Realities* (Bloomington: Indiana University Press, 1973).

5. United States, Agency for International Development, *U.S. Overseas Loans and Grants, and Assistance from International Organizations: Obligations and Loan Authorizations, July 1, 1945–September 30, 1976* (Washington, D.C.: U.S. Agency for International Development, 1976), p. 56. Total 1946–75 aid included $173.1 million in economic assistance and $26.4 million in military assistance. In addition, from 1946 to 1975, Paraguay received $288.5 million in assistance from international organizations to which the United States was a contributing member.

6. The 1943 figure is taken from United States, Department of Commerce, Office of Business Economics, *U.S. Business Investments in Foreign Countries* (Washington, D.C.: Government Printing Office, 1960), p. 92.

7. The 1975 figure was obtained by the author through personal communication with the International Investment Division of the United States Department of Commerce's Bureau of Economic Analysis, 4 January 1979. The principal nations with large-scale foreign investments in Paraguay in 1975, other than the United States, were as follows (1974 year-end figures): Argentina ($130 million), Brazil ($60 million), United Kingdom ($15 million). United States, Department of State, Foreign Affairs Document and Reference Center, *Country Fact Sheets*, vol. 4: *Inter-American Affairs* (Washington, D.C.: U.S. Department of State, 1968–), p. 4-26-16-1.

8. United States, Department of Commerce, Bureau of the Census, *Highlights of U.S. Export and Import Trade,* report FT990, December 1975 (Washington, D.C.: Government Printing Office, 1976), pp. 40, 86.

9. United States, Department of State, *Country Fact Sheets,* vol. 4: *Inter-American Affairs,* p. 4-26-20-1.

Bibliography

UNPUBLISHED RECORDS

Records of the United States Government (National Archives, Washington, D.C.)
    General Records of the Department of State (Record Group 59)
    Records of the War Department General and Special Staffs (Record Group 165)
    Records of the Foreign Economic Administration (Record Group 169)
    Records of the Joint Chiefs of Staff (Record Group 218)
    Records of the Office of Strategic Services (Record Group 226)
    Records of the Office of Inter-American Affairs (Record Group 229)
    Records of the Army Staff (Record Group 319)
Records of the Government of Great Britain (Public Record Office, London)
    Correspondence of the British Foreign Office
Manuscript Collections
    Wesley Frost Papers (Oberlin College Archives)
    Cordell Hull Papers (Library of Congress)

PUBLISHED RECORDS AND SECONDARY LITERATURE

Acheson, Dean. *Present at the Creation: My Years in the State Department.* New York: W. W. Norton & Co., Inc., 1969.
Alberto, Carlos. *Itinerario político del Paraguay, 1936–1949.* Asunción: Editorial "El País," 1950.
Alexander, Robert J. "The Latin American Aprista Parties." *Political Quarterly* 20 (July–September 1949): 236–47.
———. *The Perón Era.* New York: Columbia University Press, 1951.
Anderson, Charles W. *Politics and Economic Change in Latin America: The Governing of Restless Nations.* Princeton, N.J.: Van Nostrand Co., Inc., 1967.

Bibliography

Artaza, Policarpo. *Ayala, Estigarribia y el Partido Liberal.* Buenos Aires: Editorial Ayacucho, 1946.

Bárcena Echeviste, O. *Concepción 1947: Contribución a la historia política del Paraguay.* Buenos Aires: Juan Pellegrini, 1948.

Barclay, Glen. *Struggle for a Continent: The Diplomatic History of South America, 1917–1945.* New York: New York University Press, 1972.

Beaulac, Willard L. *Career Ambassador.* New York: Macmillan Co., 1951.

Behrendt, Richard F. *Inter-American Economic Relations: Problems and Prospects.* New York: Committee on International Economic Policy, 1948.

Bellani Nazeri, Rodolfo. *Los campos de concentración en el Paraguay.* Asunción: Editorial London F. Riolleva, 1945.

———. *Morínigo, un hombre de América.* Santiago, Chile: Editorial "Revista de las Américas," 1946.

Benítez, Justo Pastor. *Estigarribia, el soldado del Chaco.* Buenos Aires: Editorial Difusam, 1943.

Berle, Adolf Augustus. *Navigating the Rapids, 1918–1971: From the Papers of Adolf A. Berle.* Edited by Beatrice Bishop Berle and Travis Beal Jacobs. New York: Harcourt Brace Jovanovich, Inc., 1973.

Bernstein, Marvin D., ed. *Foreign Investment in Latin America: Cases and Attitudes.* New York: Alfred A. Knopf, 1966.

Black, Cyril Edwin. *The Dynamics of Modernization: A Study in Comparative History.* New York: Harper & Row, 1966.

Blanksten, George I. *Perón's Argentina.* Chicago: University of Chicago Press, 1953.

Blum, John Morton, ed. *From the Morgenthau Diaries.* 3 vols. Boston: Houghton Mifflin Co., 1959–67.

Borche, Carlos. *Campos de concentración en América (Misión en Paraguay).* Montevideo: Ediciones Patrocinadas por el Comité Nacional de Ayuda al Pueblo Paraguayo, 1945.

Bordon, F. Arturo. *Morínigo! Un paréntesis trágico en la vida democrática del Paraguay.* Asunción: Editora Tavaré, 1975.

Bourne, Richard. *Political Leaders of Latin America.* New York: Alfred A. Knopf, 1970.

Bowen, Ralph H. *German Theories of the Corporative State, with Special Reference to the Period 1870–1919.* New York: Whittlesey House, 1947.

Braden, Spruille. *Diplomats and Demagogues: The Memoirs of Spruille Braden.* New Rochelle, N.Y.: Arlington House, 1971.

———. "Latin-American Industrialization and Foreign Trade." In *Industrialization of Latin America,* edited by Lloyd J. Hughlett, pp. 486–93. New York and London: McGraw-Hill Book Co., Inc., 1946.

Burns, E. Bradford. *A History of Brazil.* New York: Columbia University Press, 1970.

Burns, James MacGregor. *Roosevelt: The Lion and the Fox.* New York: Harcourt, Brace & World, Inc., 1956.

Calleo, David P., and Rowland, Benjamin M. *America and the World Political*

Bibliography

Latin American Economic Institute. *The Economic Defense of the Western Hemisphere: A Study in Conflicts.* Washington, D.C.: American Council on Public Affairs, 1941.

Leuchtenburg, William E. *Franklin D. Roosevelt and the New Deal, 1932–1940.* New York: Harper & Row, 1963.

———. *The Perils of Prosperity, 1914–32.* Chicago: University of Chicago Press, 1958.

Levine, Robert M. *The Vargas Regime: The Critical Years, 1934–1938.* New York and London: Columbia University Press, 1970.

Lewis, Paul H. *The Politics of Exile: Paraguay's Febrerista Party.* Chapel Hill: University of North Carolina Press, 1968.

Lieuwen, Edwin. *Arms and Politics in Latin America.* New York: Frederick A. Praeger, Inc., 1961.

———. *U.S. Policy in Latin America: A Short History.* New York: Frederick A. Praeger, Inc., for the Council on Foreign Relations, 1965.

Little, Walter. "Party and State in Peronist Argentina, 1945–1955." *Hispanic American Historical Review* 53 (November 1973): 644–62.

Lott, Leo B. *Venezuela and Paraguay: Political Modernity and Tradition in Conflict.* New York: Holt, Rinehart & Winston, Inc., 1972.

McCann, Frank D., Jr. *The Brazilian-American Alliance, 1937–1945.* Princeton, N.J.: Princeton University Press, 1973.

Macias, Silvio. *Morínigo y la horda roja.* Buenos Aires: Lucania, 1947.

Malloy, James M., ed. *Authoritarianism and Corporatism in Latin America.* Pittsburgh, Pa.: University of Pittsburgh Press, 1977.

Mosk, Sanford A. "Latin America and the World Economy, 1850–1914." *Inter-American Economic Affairs* 2 (Winter 1948): 53–82.

Nolte, Ernst. *Three Faces of Fascism: Action Française, Italian Fascism, National Socialism.* Translated by Leila Vennewitz. New York: Holt, Rinehart & Winston, 1965.

Pastore, Carlos. *El Paraguay y la tirania de Morínigo.* Montevideo: Editorial Antequera, 1947.

Payne, Stanley G. *A History of Spain and Portugal.* 2 vols. Madison: University of Wisconsin Press, 1973.

Pendle, George. *Paraguay: A Riverside Nation.* 3d edition. London: Oxford University Press, for the Royal Institute of International Affairs, 1967.

Pike, Fredrick B., and Stritch, Thomas, eds. *The New Corporatism: Socio-Political Structures in the Iberian World.* Notre Dame, Ind.: University of Notre Dame Press, 1974.

Platt, Desmond Christopher St. Martin, ed. *Business Imperialism, 1840–1930: An Inquiry Based on British Experience in Latin America.* Oxford, England: Clarendon Press, 1977.

———. *Latin America and British Trade, 1806–1914.* London: Adam & Charles Black Ltd., 1972.

Potash, Robert A. *The Army and Politics in Argentina.* Vol. 1: *1928–1945.* Stanford, Calif.: Stanford University Press, 1969.

153

Bibliography

El Presidente del Paraguay y su jira de confraternidad panamericana. Buenos Aires: Talleres gráficos "Continental," 1943.

Raine, Philip. *Paraguay.* New Brunswick, N.J.: Scarecrow Press, 1956.

Reh, Emma. *Paraguayan Rural Life: Survey of Food Problems, 1943–1945.* Washington, D.C.: Institute of Inter-American Affairs, 1946.

Rich, Norman. *Hitler's War Aims.* Vol. 2: *The Establishment of the New Order.* New York: W. W. Norton & Co., Inc., 1974.

Rippy, James Fred. *British Investments in Latin America, 1822–1949: A Case Study of the Operations of Private Enterprise in Retarded Regions.* Minneapolis: University of Minnesota Press, 1959.

————. "French Investments in Latin America." *Inter-American Economic Affairs* 2 (Autumn 1948): 52–71.

————. "German Investments in Latin America." *Journal of Business of the University of Chicago* 21 (April 1948): 63–73.

————. *Globe and Hemisphere: Latin America's Place in the Postwar Foreign Relations of the United States.* Chicago: Henry Regnery Co., 1958.

————. "Italian Immigrants and Investments in Latin America." *Inter-American Economic Affairs* 3 (Autumn 1949): 25–37.

Roett, Riordan. *Brazil: Politics in a Patrimonial Society.* Boston: Allyn & Bacon, Inc., 1972.

Rogger, Hans, and Weber, Eugen, eds. *The European Right: A Historical Profile.* Berkeley and Los Angeles: University of California Press, 1965.

Romero, José Luís. *A History of Argentine Political Thought.* Translated by Thomas F. McGann. Stanford, Calif.: Stanford University Press, 1963.

Roosevelt, Franklin D. *The Public Papers and Addresses of Franklin D. Roosevelt.* Compiled by Samuel I. Rosenman. 13 vols. New York: Random House, 1938–50.

Rout, Leslie B. *Politics of the Chaco Peace Conference, 1935–39.* Austin: University of Texas Press, for the Institute of Latin American Studies, 1970.

Sammons, Robert L., and Abelson, Milton. *American Direct Investments in Foreign Countries—1940.* Bureau of Foreign and Domestic Commerce (United States Department of Commerce) Economic Series no. 20. Washington, D.C.: Government Printing Office, 1942.

Schlesinger, Arthur M., Jr. *The Crisis of the Old Order, 1919–33.* Boston: Houghton Mifflin Co., 1957.

Schuman, Frederick L. *The Nazi Dictatorship: A Study in Social Pathology and the Politics of Fascism.* 2d ed., rev. New York: Alfred A. Knopf, 1939.

Shannon, David A. *Between the Wars: America, 1919–1941.* Boston: Houghton Mifflin Co., 1965.

Simonson, William. "Nazi Infiltration in South America, 1933–1945." Ph.D. dissertation, Tufts University, 1964.

Skidmore, Thomas E. *Politics in Brazil, 1930–1964: An Experiment in Democracy.* New York: Oxford University Press, 1967.

Smith, Oscar Edmund. *Yankee Diplomacy: U.S. Intervention in Argentina.* Dallas, Tex.: Southern Methodist University Press, 1953.

Bibliography

Smith, Robert Freeman. "The Good Neighbor Policy: The Liberal Paradox in United States Relations with Latin America." In *Watershed of Empire: Essays on New Deal Foreign Policy*, edited by Leonard R. Liggio and James J. Martin. Colorado Springs, Colo.: Ralph Myles, Publisher, 1976.

Stefanich, Juan. *El Paraguay nuevo: Por la democracia y la libertad hacia un nuevo ideario americano*. Buenos Aires: Editorial Claridad, 1943.

———. *Renovación y liberación: La obra del Gobierno de Febrero*. Buenos Aires: Editorial El Mundo Nuevo, 1946.

Stein, Stanley J., and Stein, Barbara H. *The Colonial Heritage of Latin America: Essays on Economic Dependence in Perspective*. New York: Oxford University Press, 1970.

Steward, Dick. *Trade and Hemisphere: The Good Neighbor Policy and Reciprocal Trade*. Columbia: University of Missouri Press, 1975.

Trefousse, Hans Louis. *Germany and American Neutrality, 1939–1941*. New York: Bookman Associates, 1951.

United Nations. Department of Economic Affairs. *A Study of Trade between Latin America and Europe*. Geneva, Switzerland: United Nations, 1953.

———. Department of Economic and Social Affairs. *Foreign Capital in Latin America*. New York: United Nations, 1955.

United States. Agency for International Development. *U.S. Overseas Loans and Grants, and Assistance from International Organizations: Obligations and Loan Authorizations, July 1, 1945–September 30, 1976*. Washington, D.C.: U.S. Agency for International Development, 1976.

———. Department of Commerce. Bureau of Foreign and Domestic Commerce. *Foreign Commerce Yearbook, 1933–51*. Washington, D.C.: Government Printing Office, 1934–52.

———. ———. Bureau of Foreign Commerce. *Investment in Paraguay: Conditions and Outlook for United States Investors*. Washington, D.C.: Government Printing Office, 1955.

———. ———. Bureau of the Census. *Highlights of U.S. Export and Import Trade*. Report FT990, December 1975. Washington, D.C.: Government Printing Office, 1976.

———. ———. Office of Business Economics. *U.S. Business Investments in Foreign Countries*. Washington, D.C.: Government Printing Office, 1960.

———. Department of State. *Consultation among the American Republics with Respect to the Argentine Situation*. Washington, D.C.: Government Printing Office, 1946.

———. ———. *Documents on German Foreign Policy, 1918–1945*. Series D, 13 vols. Washington, D.C.: Government Printing Office, 1949–64.

———. ———. *Foreign Relations of the United States, 1938–1948*. Washington, D.C.: Government Printing Office, 1958–72.

———. ———. *Private Enterprise in the Development of the Americas: An Address by Assistant Secretary Braden before the Executives' Club of Chicago, September 13, 1946*. Inter-American Series, no. 32. Washington, D.C.: Government Printing Office, 1946.

Bibliography

————. ————. *Report of the Delegate of the United States of America to the Meeting of the Foreign Ministers of the American Republics Held at Panama, September 23–October 3, 1939.* Washington, D.C.: Government Printing Office, 1940.

————. ————. *Report of the Delegates of the United States of America to the Seventh International Conference of American States, Montevideo, Uruguay, December 3–26, 1933.* Washington, D.C.: Government Printing Office, 1934.

————. ————. *Report of the Delegation of the United States of America to the Eighth International Conference of American States, Lima, Peru, December 9–27, 1938.* Washington, D.C.: Government Printing Office, 1941.

————. ————. *Report of the Delegation of the United States of America to the Inter-American Conference on Problems of War and Peace, Mexico City, Mexico, February 21–March 8, 1945.* Washington, D.C.: Government Printing Office, 1946.

————. ————. *Second Meeting of the Ministers of Foreign Affairs of the American Republics, Habana, July 21–30, 1940, Report of the Secretary of State.* Washington, D.C.: Government Printing Office, 1941.

————. ————. Foreign Affairs Document and Reference Center. *Country Fact Sheets. Vol. 4: Inter-American Affairs.* Washington, D.C.: U.S. Department of State, 1968–.

Varg, Paul A. "The Economic Side of the Good Neighbor Policy: The Reciprocal Trade Program and South America." *Pacific Historical Review* 45 (February 1976): 47–71.

Villasboa, Mutshuito. *Hacia la guerra total y los problemas de las fuerzas armadas.* Asunción: Biblioteca de Las Fuerzas Armadas de la Nación, n.d.

Warren, Carlos A. *Emancipación económica americana.* Montevideo: Editorial Ceibo, 1946.

Warren, Harris Gaylord. *Paraguay: An Informal History.* Norman: University of Oklahoma Press, 1949.

————. "Political Aspects of the Paraguayan Revolution, 1936–1940." *Hispanic American Historical Review* 30 (February 1950): 2–25.

Watson, Mark Skinner. *Chief of Staff: Prewar Plans and Preparations.* Vol. 4, pt. 1, of *United States Army in World War II,* edited by Kent Roberts Greenfield. Washington, D.C.: Government Printing Office, 1950.

Weber, Eugen J. *Varieties of Fascism: Doctrines of Revolution in the Twentieth Century.* Princeton, N.J.: Van Nostrand Co., Inc., 1964.

Weinstein, Martin. *Uruguay: The Politics of Failure.* Westport, Conn.: Greenwood Press, 1975.

Welles, Sumner. *The Time for Decision.* Cleveland and New York: World Publishing Co., 1945.

————. *Where Are We Heading?* New York and London: Harper & Bros., 1946.

Williams, John Hoyt. "Paraguay's Nineteenth-Century *Estancias de la República.*" *Agricultural History* 47 (July 1973): 206–15.

Bibliography

Williams, Margaret Todaro. "Integralism and the Brazilian Catholic Church." *Hispanic American Historical Review* 54 (August 1974): 431–52.

Wirth, John D. *The Politics of Brazilian Development, 1930–1954*. Stanford, Calif.: Stanford University Press, 1970.

Wood, Bryce. *The Making of the Good Neighbor Policy*. New York: W. W. Norton & Co., 1967.

Woolf, S. J., ed. *The Nature of Fascism*. New York: Random House, 1968.

Wythe, George. *Industry in Latin America*. 2d ed. New York: Columbia University Press, 1949.

Ynsfran, Edgar L. *La irrupción moscovita en la Marina Paraguaya*. Asunción: privately printed, 1947.

Zook, David H., Jr. *The Conduct of the Chaco War*. New York: Bookman Associates, 1960.

INTERVIEWS AND CORRESPONDENCE

Willard Beaulac, personal interview, Washington, D.C., 20 January 1975.

Higinio Morínigo, letter to author, 12 March 1975.

Index

Andrada, Carlos, 61, 62, 76. *See also* Tiempistas

Aranda, Bernardo, 61, 134 n.7. *See also* Frente de guerra

Argaña, Luis, 61, 65, 70, 75–76, 78, 138 n.4. *See also* Tiempistas

Argentina: impact of Depression on, 17; fascism in, 18; authoritarian nationalism in, 19–23 passim, 70, 94–96, 98, 123 n.18, 138 n.4; trade relations of, 27–31, 86, 88–90, 124 n.1; and U.S., 28–29, 31, 38, 39, 69–70, 86, 88–89, 95–96, 98, 124 n.1, 138 n.4; Germans in, 33, 34–35, 126 n.16; at 1938 Lima Conference, 38, 39; at 1942 Rio Conference, 69–70; and 1947 Paraguayan civil war, 147 n.27

Armed forces, 18, 33, 36, 40, 129 n.10. *See also* Paraguay: armed forces of; Brazil: army of

Asunción Port Concession Corporation, 45, 64

Authoritarianism, 1–2, 18–23, 32–33, 39–40, 94–95. *See also* Argentina: authoritarian nationalism in; Brazil: authoritarian nationalism in; Paraguay: authoritarian nationalism in; Uruguay: authoritarian nationalism in

Aviation, 79–81, 90, 106

Ayala, Eusebio, 48, 130 n.15

Ayala, Juan B., 70

Beaulac, Willard, 102–4, 106–7, 108, 144 n.10, 146 n.27

Behrens, Reimer, 52

Benítez, Justo Pastor, 130–31 n.24

Benítez Vera, Victoriano, 61, 78, 80. *See also* Frente de guerra

Berle, Adolf, 97

Bolivia, 54–55, 124 n.1, 129 n.10, 136 n.23, 138 n.4

Braden, Spruille, 91–92, 95–98, 146 n.27

Brazil: impact of Depression on, 17; fascism in, 18; authoritarian nationalism in, 19–23 passim, 94–98 passim; trade relations of, 26–31, 86, 88–89, 124 n.1; and U.S., 26, 28–29, 31, 40–41, 86, 88–89, 96–98, 117–18, 124 n.1, 128 n.39, 143 n.44; and Germany, 27–31, 40–41, 86, 88–89; Germans in, 33, 34–35, 126 n.16; army of, 40, 97–98, 142 n.42; and 1942 Rio Conference, 69

Brugada Doldán, Ricardo, 65

Byrnes, James F., 91

Cabot, John, 96, 141 n.34

Campos, Francisco, 21

Carlos Casado, Ltd., 45

Castillo, Ramón, 69

Catholic Church, 15, 18–19, 51, 122 n.7, 147 n.29

Central Intelligence Agency (U.S.), 146 n.27

Chaco War, 46, 47, 50, 59, 129 n.10

Chaves, Federico, 107, 108, 110

Collado, Emilio, 56, 75, 137 n.2

Colorado party, 44–48 passim, 50, 63, 105–

DATE DUE

31Oct83			
GAYLORD			PRINTED IN U.S.A.